LECTURES ON
GENERAL PSYCHOLOGY

~ VOLUME TWO ~

LECTURES ON GENERAL PSYCHOLOGY

~ Volume Two ~

Dennis Ford

Lectures on General Psychology ~ Volume Two

iUniverse books may be ordered through booksellers or by contacting:

iUniverse
1663 Liberty Drive
Bloomington, IN 47403
www.iuniverse.com
1-800-Authors (1-800-288-4677)

ISBN: 978-1-4917-7946-0 (sc)
ISBN: 978-1-5320-2983-7 (hc)
ISBN: 978-1-4917-7945-3 (e)

Library of Congress Control Number: 2015953742

Print information available on the last page.

iUniverse rev. date: 08/07/2017

Also by Dennis Ford

Fiction
Red Star
Landsman
Things Don't Add Up

Humor
Thinking About Everything
Miles of Thoughts

Family History
Genealogical Jaunts
Eight Generations

to twenty five years of students

and to the memory of my Mother,
my first and most important teacher

TABLE OF CONTENTS

PREFACE

In *Thinking About Everything* (entry forty eight) I expressed the insight that our thoughts and experiences will be permanently lost unless we write them down or record them in some way. This insight was a sensible suggestion. It may even have been a sagacious suggestion. And it was a suggestion I did not keep.

For twenty five years I've taught general psychology at the Borough of Manhattan Community College at Chambers St. in Lower Manhattan. That's fifty courses and two thousand students. I came recently to the disturbing realization that there is no permanent record of the twelve lectures I dutifully delivered semester after semester. The only records of the lectures were in the irretrievable notebooks of dispersed students and the cryptic bullet points I outlined on coffee-stained scratch paper. All the good lines delivered in the lectures were in my head—that was a dangerous place for them to be.

I risked losing twenty five years of psychological observations and principles. I couldn't let that happen.

I decided in 2014 to write the lectures word-for-word as I delivered them and then to publish them. This was a way to preserve the lectures and to keep them from sailing to the land of oblivion. The twelve lectures are contained in this volume and in *Volume One*. The lectures are in the order I presented them. Grammar has been added—speech is sloppy and lacks punctuation—but the content is the same as I delivered in class. Everything I said is now on paper—the material is safe now and preserved. The same definitions. The same examples. The same jokes. The same throw-away lines. The same witticisms. The same insights. The same shrewd observations. The same sage advice. Or so I like to think.

Someone once remarked that teachers are the last vaudevillians. Writing the lectures brought home the truth in that observation. The classroom is my stage. The students are my audience. The blackboard is my set. The chalk is my prop. The lectures are my shtick. After twenty five years I know exactly what works. I know the places in the lectures where I get the students' full attention. I know the places where I lose their attention—this usually happens a half hour before the act ends. I know the places where I shock and surprise the students. I know the places where I bore them. I know the places where they get upset and become earnest. I know the places where they laugh. I know the places where they groan. The groaning doesn't bother me. It's precisely the reaction I expect.

The twelve lectures contain a critical presentation of a selection of mainstream topics in general psychology. For a full exploration of the wonders of psychology the lectures should be read in conjunction with a first course general psychology textbook that covers the same topics. Over the years I used a number of textbooks that are compatible with the volumes of *Lectures on General Psychology*. In former years the textbooks included Bourne and Ekstrand's *Psychology: Its Principles and Meaning*, Lindzey, Hall and Thompson's *Psychology*, and Whittaker's *Introduction to Psychology*. In recent years I favored *Exploring Psychology* by David G. Myers.

Following each lecture I've included a selection of "Tips to Students." These are suggested practices based on psychological principles that, if applied, can facilitate learning the material covered in the lectures. I firmly believe that studying is a skill analogous to throwing a baseball or to surfing. The more students learn the correct methods of study, the better they will get at studying and the greater their performance in class and on quizzes.

I take full responsibility for any errors and for any misjudgments in the applications of psychological principles. As I wrote in *Thinking About Everything* (entry one hundred eighteen), there is no shame in making a mistake. The only shame is having to admit I made one.

OVERVIEW OF THE LECTURES

Lecture One describes the method of studying sleep in "sleep laboratories." Physiological and psychological processes occurring in REM (rapid eye movement) sleep and NREM (no rapid eye movement) sleep are compared. The stages of delta brain waves in NREM sleep are outlined. The sleep cycle is outlined. Phenomena that occur in sleep are described. The concept of a "sleep ritual" is introduced. Individual differences and changes in sleep across the life span are reviewed. The effects of sleep deprivation (sleep debt) are explored. The leading causes of insomnia are described, as are ways to avoid insomnia. Differences between dreams in REM sleep and in NREM sleep are outlined. Retroactive interference is described as the reason we fail to remember dreams. Tips on how to remember dreams are provided.

Lecture Two reviews the concept of motivation in the history of psychology. This review includes instinct theory, homeostasis, and learning psychology. Learning principles include positive and negative reinforcement, incentives, shifts in reward, the matching law, and intrinsic and extrinsic reinforcement. Maslow's five level hierarchy of needs is outlined. Hunger and eating are analyzed as a typical motive. The physiological, neuronal, psychological, and social-cultural factors that interact to activate and satisfy hunger are explored. The factors responsible for the eating disorders of anorexia nervosa, bulimia nervosa, and obesity are outlined. Factors that facilitate and complicate dieting are described.

Lecture Three reviews some of the difficulties studying emotions. The universality of the basic emotions is described. The relationship of arousal to performance is outlined. Problems in the use of the polygraph machine in the detection of lies are reviewed. Characteristics of the emotion of anger are examined. The Type A personality is described, as is the deadly effect of anger on the cardio-vascular system. Catharsis is defined and debunked. The sources of happiness are reviewed. The principles of adaptation level and relative deprivation are described in relation to happiness. The original and the revised James-Lange theory of emotion are outlined. The role of facial displays in emotion and the facial modulation of emotion are described.

Lecture Four introduces the subfield of health psychology, which applies the principles of psychology to the states of sickness and wellness. Wellness is defined as a dynamic state that is not merely the absence of disease. Stress is considered as a major factor in sickness and in wellness. Stress is defined as the physiological and psychological reaction to the demands life places on us. The origins of stress lie in the experience of daily hassles, life changes, and catastrophes. The effects of stress on the body are examined. Factors that worsen or ameliorate the effects of stress are reviewed. These factors are individual differences in the appraisal and interpretation of stress, personality factors, the predictability of the onset and offset of stress, the presence of social support, coping mechanisms, socioeconomic factors, and the control or perceived control of the sources of stress.

Lecture Five defines social roles and contrasts them with concepts in personality theories. Zimbardo's "Stanford prison study" is reviewed. Attribution theory is introduced. The fundamental attribution error is described, as is the self-serving bias and the just-world phenomenon. Conformity and groupthink are described. Obedience is examined in the context of Milgram's notorious experiment using fake shock. The concepts of conformity and obedience are used to demonstrate the situational orientation of social psychology. Social psychological variables that underlie liking and altruism are examined. The belief, feeling, and behavior components of attitudes are described. Cognitive dissonance is defined. Changing behavior through manipulating cognitive dissonance is described. Social psychological factors that influence the attitude of prejudice are outlined.

Lecture Six discusses the difficulties in defining psychological disorders. The suggestion is advanced that psychological disorders are exaggerations and caricatures of normal human behavior. The importance and dangers of diagnosis are described. Diagnosis on the basis of six perspectives is discussed. These perspectives are the neuroscience, behavioral, cognitive, psychodynamic, behavior genetics, and social-cultural perspectives. Diagnosis on the basis of symptoms using the Diagnostic and Statistical Manual (DSM 5) is outlined. Clinical psychology and psychiatry are distinguished, as are organic and functional disorders. Four categories of disorder are reviewed. These categories are anxiety disorders (phobic disorder and post-traumatic stress disorder), mood disorders (major depression and bipolar disorder), personality disorders (paranoid type, antisocial type, and narcissistic type), and thought disorders (schizophrenia). Hallucinations and delusions are described as symptoms of schizophrenia. The central experience of schizophrenia is defined as a loss of control of awareness.

LECTURE ONE ~
Sleep and Dreams

Throughout history human beings have been sleeping. Consider what the Hebrew Testament says. Adam fell asleep and God took a rib and made Eve—it's been downhill ever since. In the Christian Testament a few thousand years after Adam and Eve the apostles were asleep in the Garden of Gethsemane when Jesus had his crises. So there, it's proven. People have been sleeping all along.

People have been interested in dreams throughout recorded history. I suppose they have been interested in dreams throughout unrecorded history as well. We don't know what Adam was dreaming when God took the rib. We like to think it was something positive. The apostles were likely dreaming of divvying up God's Kingdom among themselves. In the Hebrew Testament Joseph got paid good money to interpret Pharaoh's dream of the seven fat calves followed by the seven lean calves. In the Christian Testament an angel appeared in the dream of a different Joseph and advised him to get out of town and to take Mary and the Infant Jesus with him.

Consider that we spend one third of our lives asleep. If we live to be thirty, that's ten full years in the land of Nod. If we live to be ninety, that's thirty full years. That's a lifetime spent in Nod. We shouldn't hold this against Gramps. Sleep is not time wasted, as you will soon hear.

My point in this kind of introduction is the following. People have been asleep and dreaming, but it was only in the 1950s that sleep was studied under controlled scientific conditions. It's baffling that scientists waited so long to study what happens to the body and to the mind when we pass through customs in Nod—the customs officer on duty is named Murphy. No one knows his personal name.

In 1953 Eugene Aserinsky paid University of Chicago students to sleep in a "sleep laboratory." This is the opposite of what sometimes happens in this school, where a few students pay us and sleep in class. Many universities and hospitals have "sleep labs" and "sleep clinics" where people with sleep disorders and brain problems can be observed. Aserinsky's sleep lab was among the first. Quite an original and—after thousands of years—a timely concept.

Aserinsky and his colleagues attached three nonintrusive monitors to the scalps of the students so that the activity of the body could be tracked throughout sleep. The activity going on in the mind was tracked by waking the students up periodically and asking what was on their minds. Were they dreaming or not?

The three machines that monitored the body were the electrooculograph (EOG), the electromylograph (EMG), and the electroencephalograph (EEG). The electrooculograph monitors the movements of the muscles of the eyes. The electromylograph monitors muscle tone—how tight are the muscles of the scalp. And the electroencephalograph monitors the brain wave activity of millions of neurons in the occipital lobes of the brain.

Using a readout of these machines Aserinsky and his colleagues discovered that we have two different kinds of sleep and that we experience a sleep cycle that alternates between the two.

This information was not known to Adam—we like to think God knew it. This information was not known to both Josephs. Sigmund Freud didn't know it. Carl Gustav Jung didn't know it. Alfred Adler didn't know it. No psychologist knew this before 1953. This lack of information didn't stop psychologists famous and un-famous from writing about dreams. But that's a different lecture.

The two kinds of sleep are *REM sleep—rapid eye movement sleep—* and *NREM sleep—no rapid eye movement sleep*. REM sleep is also called *paradoxical sleep* for a reason I'll explain shortly. NREM is also called *quiet sleep*. Unless something bad happens in the meanwhile, I'll explain that, too. REM and NREM involve different states of the body. And they involve different kinds of dreams.

REM sleep is a unitary, non-differentiated state. Sleepers are either in REM or not in REM. There are no states or levels of REM. NREM is differentiated into four states or levels. These levels are defined by the presence and the amount of *delta brain wave activity*. When we sleep, we fly delta.

As you recall, neurons give off electrical impulses. Firings of hundreds of thousands of neurons result in identifiable patterns of electrical activities called *brain waves*. Brain waves are assessed, like all waves, on the basis of frequency and amplitude.

Beta brain waves are found in the alert, awake, thinking and processing brain. This is the state students are in as they listen to the lecture and think about the topic.

Back in the 1960s and 1970s *alpha brain waves* became notorious when it was discovered that people who regularly meditate show increased levels of alpha brain waves. It was thought alpha brain waves were associated with Nirvana, so a lot of people started pursuing alpha brain waves. Eastern sages achieved alpha brain waves through years devoted to meditation. Practical Americans wanted to enter Nirvana on the quick and easy. Machines were manufactured and offered for sale that monitored brain waves in the same way machines monitored pulse and blood pressure. Scientifically, this endeavor was called *biofeedback*. Psychologically, it involved applying operant conditioning procedures to increase the rate of alpha brain waves. Religiously, this endeavor was a case of pride—and a case of sloth. People who purchased the machines were separated from their money and remained earthbound on the wheel of karma.

Alpha brain waves occur when we are not focusing on anything or thinking about anything in particular. They might occur when we are drowsing on the D train or when we are sprawled on a beach chair at Coney Island. I don't doubt they sometimes occur in Prof. Ford's class.

Delta brain waves are low frequency, high amplitude waves that never occur in the awake brain. They most assuredly do not occur in Prof. Ford's class, as they occur only in NREM sleep and when a person is in a coma. Please don't confuse NREM sleep with being in a coma.

There are four stages of NREM sleep. The stages are defined by the presence and amount of delta brain waves. *Stage One* has no delta waves. *Stage Two* has less than 20% delta. That is, less than 20% of the total brain wave patterns observed on the EEG are delta waves. *Stage Three* has 20% – 50% delta. *Stage Four* has more than 50% delta. That is, more than 50% of the total brain wave patterns observed are delta waves.

The important point to remember is that the greater the percentage of delta brain waves, the deeper the sleep. Stage One is light sleep. Stage Four is deepest sleep. Probably, Adam was in Stage Four when God took the rib.

Overall, NREM sleep accounts for 75% of the total time spent asleep. REM sleep accounts for 25%. Of the four stages of NREM, Stage Two accounts for 50% of the time spent asleep. We are in Stage Two of NREM sleep half the time we are asleep.

Sleep is a biological need. If we don't sleep, we eventually die. Sleep is also a learned habit. We learn when, where, and how to sleep. Humans are a daytime species. But approximately 20% of Americans work at night and sleep by day. Those students who have night jobs know how difficult it is to sleep during the day. Some people, like police officers, work in shifts—8:00 AM to 4:00 PM, 4:00 PM to midnight; midnight to 8:00 AM. This kind of schedule is very difficult to adjust to, because sleep is a habit and we can't form a habit when the hours given to sleep change weekly. Maybe shift work is why police officers are always in bad moods.

New York use to boast that it is "the city that never sleeps." This must be the reason why New Yorkers are cranky and ill-tempered—they're dazed and tired.

Years ago, I worked as a dispatcher for a firm that hauled garments from New Jersey to California. The truck drivers would drive for ten hours, sleep for four, drive for ten, sleep for four, drive for ten—and crash. I can advise you to change lanes if you see an eighteen-wheeler barreling down in the rearview mirror. The driver is probably dazed and tired. If you're lucky, he's not dozing.

As we'll see, the lack of sleep is no small matter. Being dazed and tired is not a safe state to be in.

Everyone has a *sleep ritual* they engage in before they fall asleep. Some people watch a favorite television show—they're in trouble if the show goes off the air. Other people like to read a book. Other people like to munch on milk and cookies. Other people like to mellow out with an alcoholic beverage—this may not be such a good practice. Other people pray. Other people make love. Some people sleep on their left side. Other people sleep on their right side. Other people like to lie on their bellies. Other people like to lie flat on their backs. As we start to slide into unconsciousness we put ourselves in a favorite fantasy. I'm not going to tell you my fantasy, because you'll lose respect for me. Besides, you have your own fantasies to deal with.

All right, we watched our favorite show, we read a book, we munched on milk and cookies, we knocked back a belt or two, we said our prayers, and we made love. We're in our favorite fantasy. And we're out. We're officially asleep. There's no perceptible change in the electroencephalogram to document the exact moment we enter sleep. Once we're asleep, we progress through the *sleep cycle*. There is a progressive slowing of brain waves—this slowing is an increase in delta waves. We progress through NREM sleep—Stage One, Stage Two, Stage Three, Stage Four. We then progress back—Stage Four, Stage Three, Stage Two, Stage One. At this point we enter the first REM period. This REM period is brief. We then return to NREM sleep and progress through the stages—Stage One, Stage Two, Stage Three, Stage Four, and then in reverse Stage Four, Stage Three, Stage Two, Stage One. We then enter the next REM period. This period is a little longer than the first. We then return to NREM, but now NREM sleep is not as deep. Maybe Stage Four drops out. Stage Three reduces in duration. And there's increased REM sleep. This cycle of NREM sleep becoming lighter and REM sleep growing longer continues for as long as we sleep. It occurs if we sleep in the nighttime. It occurs if we sleep in the daytime.

This is an important point to remember about the sleep cycle—our deepest sleep happens early in the sleep cycle and soon after we fall asleep. The longer we sleep, the less deep sleep is.

Students have asked, "Professor, you have the appearance of knowing everything—that's what you tell us. If we party to the early hours, should we stay awake or should we try to catch a few hours of sleep before we come to class?" This is not a difficult one to answer. Since our deepest sleep occurs soon after we fall asleep, I advise the students to get some shut eye. A few hours of sleep are better than no sleep.

Another important point to remember is this—the longer we sleep, the more REM sleep we have. If we sleep for a long while, the chances are good we'll wake up in REM sleep. As you'll hear shortly,

REM sleep is characterized by the old-fashioned strange dreams we love and sometimes fear to experience. If we sleep for a long while, we'll experience the longest and strangest dreams right before we wake up. These are the dreams we tend to remember. It's like walking into a movie at the climax. We missed all the earlier scenes. They may be just as exciting, but we don't know that.

REM sleep is called "paradoxical sleep" because the brain is fully alert and the body is thoroughly unresponsive. We should be awake, but we're sound asleep. If we took a printout of brain wave activity in REM sleep and compared it to a printout of brain wave activity at this moment when we're presumably fully awake and alert, we couldn't tell the difference. Brain waves in REM sleep resemble brain waves of full wakefulness. But we're sound asleep. And our bodies are thoroughly unresponsive to what the brain is commanding.

There are a few well-known experiences that occur in sleep. Some people experience the sensation of falling and of jerking into wakefulness immediately after falling asleep. In case you need to know—like on a game show or on a quiz—the scientific name for this sensation is *myoclonia*. A myoclonia is a startle reflex experienced under the condition of sleep. If a truck backfires while we're awake, we may open our eyes a little wider, but we don't exhibit a startle reflex. In sleep the cerebral cortex is less vigilant, so a startle will be experienced more intensely.

There's an old wives' tale told about hitting bottom in a myoclonia and subsequently dying. We don't know with absolute certainty that this doesn't happen, because the people who hit bottom and died didn't wake up to tell us. But there are people who hit bottom and lived. They just get up, dust themselves off, and carry on with sleep. If you're worried about hitting bottom, you can wear a parachute to bed. When you feel yourself falling, pull the ripcord. This may inconvenience the person you're sleeping with. You better warn him or her ahead of time. They may experience a genuine startle as they hit the floor.

Another phenomenon that occurs just after we fall asleep is that some people experience *hypnagogic reveries*. This wonderful nineteenth century word—they knew how to make up words in the nineteenth century—describes a series of vivid disconnected images that appear in the mind. They are not coherent images and they are not like dreams.

People who experience them say they're like the images on a television screen when a person changes stations rapidly. The experience sounds odd, but the people who experience these reveries say that they like them.

Some people experience these images shortly before waking up. When they happen at that time, they're called *hypnopompic reveries*. That's another grand nineteenth century term.

There are other, better known, phenomena that occur in sleep. These occur in deepest NREM sleep—Stages Three and Four. They are sleep walking, sleep talking, bed wetting, and nocturnal emissions. Bed wetting can be a serious problem in a small percentage of boys. I suppose so can nocturnal emissions.

Should we wake up a person who's sleep walking? There's no reason why we shouldn't. The person is sleeping. They're not going to collapse. They're not going to die. We like to think not, anyway. Just wake them up gently and guide them back to bed. Take the turkey leg out of their hands first—perhaps you remember Ed Norton's jaunts to the refrigerator in a *Honeymooners* episode.

Those of you who are parents know that children do odd things in sleep and wind up in strange places as they blaze a trail through quiet sleep. They wander into the living room, they wander into the garden, they wander onto the fire escape, and all the while they're sound asleep. On occasion, they even wander into the parents' bed. And they don't know how they got there.

I'll like now to compare and contrast REM and NREM.

There is a low state of muscle tension in REM sleep. Our muscle tone is so low we are effectively paralyzed. This is a good thing or we'd be acting out our dreams. One time a student told me that her REM dream was so weird she started running around the bedroom. She would have climbed the walls, but there's something called gravity that kept her from doing that. I gently corrected her, but I thought, "Liar. You can't run around the room, still less climb the walls as you are effectively paralyzed in REM sleep."

Low muscle tone may be responsible for some of the weirdness of REM dreams. We're being chased in a dream. We seem to be running, but there's no feedback from the legs. We're in a fight—there's no feedback from the arms. We're in the water and swimming, but there's no feedback from the body roll.

This low muscle tone may be responsible for the strange experience people have of waking up and being unable to move. Some people report a heavy sensation, as if something lay on their chests. One student, an animal lover, said it felt like a cat was sitting on her. Another student, a religious person, said it felt like Satan was sitting on her. I told her the sensation was not Satan but REM sleep, but I don't think she believed me. I think she preferred it was Satan.

We have normal muscle tone in NREM. We can do anything in NREM as when we are awake—this may not be too impressive for some people. We can talk and be understood. We can walk. We can lash out. We can kick. We can pull the covers over our heads. We can throw the covers off the bed. We can pull the ripcord and land safely. Some people are more active in NREM sleep than when they are awake. Whoever said sleep was like death—as in the "big sleep"—or when we say a corpse "looks like he's asleep" never took a psychology class.

We can hear the difference between NREM and REM. When we talk in NREM we can be understood. Our mouth muscles move normally. So be careful what you say. Our dream conversations can be held against us. In REM sleep the muscles of the mouth and jaw are clamped and sealed tight. When we talk in REM it sounds like we're talking under our breaths or with our mouths closed. We can't be understood. If we're going to say something that can incriminate us, we better say it in REM sleep.

In REM sleep our autonomic nervous system is aroused. Our heart rate changes, our blood pressure changes, our lung capacity changes. In NREM sleep our autonomic nervous system is quiescent. There's steady heart rate, steady blood pressure, steady breathing. This is why NREM sleep is called "quiet sleep"—there's not much going on physiologically in comparison to REM sleep.

Genital arousal occurs as part of this autonomic nervous system activity in REM. Men get erections, women get moist. Notice I didn't say "sexual arousal." This arousal occurs whatever we are dreaming of. The sexual connotation happens because genital arousal occurs in REM sleep and the longer we stay asleep, the more likely we are to be in REM when we wake up. We wake up in a state of genital arousal and we put two and two together and before we know it we're hauling our spouses off the floor.

To the contrary, there is no genital arousal in NREM sleep. If we wake up in quiet sleep and want to become sexually aroused, the onus is on us. We have to do all the work.

The defining characteristic of these states of sleep is the kind of eye movements involved. Rapid eye movements. No rapid eye movements. Unless a person is dreaming of a ping pong match, the rapid eye movements do not correspond to the content of the dreams a person experiences. They're of the order of autonomic twitches than anything deliberate or cognitive.

The eye movements in quiet sleep are of the order of long slow rolling eye movements. Be careful if you sleep on your back. An old wife once told me that, if we're not careful, our eyes can roll around and see the inside of our heads. I had to refill her flask to make the correction.

We can dream at any moment in sleep. But we are more likely to remember the dreams we experience in paradoxical sleep. Maybe that's because we are more likely to wake up in paradoxical sleep. And maybe that's because paradoxical sleep dreams are more vivid and bizarre than dreams in quiet sleep.

Paradoxical sleep dreams are the vivid, emotional, and bizarre dreams we know and love. Sometimes we know and fear them. They don't make sense. They don't correspond with reality. Last night I dreamed I came to school and stabbed the academic dean with a straw I took from a Komodo dragon in the cafeteria. Okay, I made this dream up, but I could have dreamed it in paradoxical sleep.

Dreams in quiet sleep are more like ordinary thinking. They're not especially emotional or bizarre. They make sense. They correspond with reality. Last night I dreamed I came to school and got a coffee from the cafeteria. Then I came upstairs and took a quiz—this dream may be a nightmare. But it could have happened in quiet sleep. It's ordinary. It's realistic.

Some people experience *nightmares*. These are vivid dreams in paradoxical sleep that include frightening images and intense negative emotions. A number of conditions can inspire nightmares—to name a few, a stressful lifestyle, strong emotions, a change in sleep patterns, discontinuing alcohol or sleeping pills as part of the sleep ritual.

Night terrors are a comparable condition to nightmares that occur in NREM sleep. These occur in childhood and become less common as we mature. In night terrors a child starts to scream and to demonstrate great fear and terror. Usually, the child cannot articulate the cause of the terror. The child is pacified after a while and goes back to sleep. The following morning the child wakes up and may not remember the incident. The entire family woke up, the entire apartment building woke up, the entire South Bronx woke up—and the child goes back to bed and gets up properly refreshed the next morning.

As with nightmares, there is no single cause for night terrors. They may result from stress. They may result from the overload of learning on the child's nervous system. They may also result from a quirk of personality. For whatever reason, some children are prone to night terrors. The good news is that children generally grow out of them by adolescence.

It is not known why we sleep. It is not fatigue. It is not lack of sensory stimulation—people who live in sensory-deprived conditions find it difficult to fall asleep. It is not the need for healing or to repair the rips and rends that flesh is heir to. Perhaps sleep serves a defensive function. Predators can't tear us from limb to limb when we are holed up in cozy caves. Perhaps sleep is a way to conserve energy. Perhaps sleep plays a role in the consolidation and reorganization of thoughts and memories.

Sleep is a biological need, but there are wide individual differences in how much sleep we need and in how we react to sleep deprivation. There are people who function well with just a few hours sleep. There are other people who require eight and ten hours of sleep to function as citizens in the state of wellness.

There has never been a case of a person who didn't sleep. There was a man who lived on Columbus Ave. who claimed he never slept, but secret cameras recorded him snoring loudly on a nightly basis. The longest documented case of a person staying awake was Randy Gardner, a California teen who stayed awake for two hundred sixty four hours for a charity event. This is eleven days rounding off. He was not psychologically affected and could do everything at eleven days he could do on day one—with one exception. He couldn't sit still or lie down or he would go instantly to sleep. He had to keep moving to keep awake.

Randy Gardner must have been a blessed individual. Despite the lack of sleep, he could play billiards better than one of the scientists observing him. This was the wonderfully named Dr. William Dement. The fact that a sleep-deprived teen could beat him at billiards doesn't speak well of Dr. Dement's athletic ability.

After his ordeal Randy went to bed and slept for seventeen hours. He got up, yawned, stretched, had breakfast, and, since that was California, went skateboarding on the Boardwalk. During this sleep Randy experienced a pronounced increase in REM sleep. This is referred to as the "REM rebound." It occurs in people who do not get the right amount of sleep and the right amount of REM. This REM rebound can be associated with nightmares. As we might expect, the more REM we have the greater the risk of nightmares. If not of nightmares, then of weird dreams.

There are individual differences in the amount of sleep we need. There are individual differences in the amount of sleep we need— and get—across our life spans. Babies sleep more than adolescents. Adolescents sleep more than adults. Middle-aged people sleep more than senior citizens.

Babies sleep sixteen hours a day, but not all in one period. It takes a year or longer for babies to sleep through the night and stay awake through the day. As parents know, some babies have a lot of trouble associating sleep with night and darkness.

Babies have a lot more REM sleep than adults. Fifty percent of the total sleep cycle is REM sleep in babies compared to the amount adults have, which is roughly 25%. The older people are, the less sleep they experience and the less REM sleep they have. Babies can enter REM sleep immediately on falling asleep, which is something the normal adult brain cannot do. Some people believe that REM sleep plays a role in brain development. Most everything babies experience is new. Neural pathways are constantly being laid down in babies. The brain is busily wiring and rewiring itself in infancy compared to what goes on in adulthood.

Sleep is an important process that contributes to health and to wellness, not to mention to creativity and to good scores on psychology quizzes. It is an unfortunate fact of our civilized lives in the last remaining superpower that we do not get enough sleep. Overall, Americans sleep an average of one less hour in 2010 than we did in 1980. We have learned to function deprived of the full amount of sleep we require on a daily basis. We have learned to function groggy. We have learned to function feeling tired. We make mistakes. We're not as creative as we might otherwise be. We gain weight. We don't score as high as we ought to on quizzes. We get sick. We crack up. We get injured in automobile crashes. As I say, sleep is an important part of our lives.

A recent concept in sleep research is *sleep debt*. This is the amount of hours of sleep we need but do not get. Sleep debt is what we owe the Sandman.

Many people, myself included, try to pay the debt by sleeping late one day of the week. If I may be permitted to self disclose, I pay my debt on Sundays, when I stay under the sheets till nine AM. The rest of the week I'm up early and stay awake late. This strategy of sleeping late one day makes sense and I suppose it's the only thing we can do, but it doesn't work and it may backfire. Besides being a biological need, sleep is a habit—I think I said this. Getting up early and staying up late six days a week and then sleeping late one day is hardly conducive to a restful pattern. It is rather an erratic way of doing business.

Loss of sleep is a serious matter. It's estimated that there are thousands of injuries in car crashes and fifteen hundred deaths a year because people fall asleep driving or are so tired they can't react promptly. It happens all the time in my country of New Jersey. I read in the paper that Mr. So-and-So died in a single car crash on the Garden State Parkway. No one can figure out what caused So-and-So to drive into the woods. A likely explanation is that he fell asleep. Another explanation is that couldn't react fast enough when a deer leaped across the road. At seventy miles an hour a quarter inch movement on the steering wheel can get a car sandwiched in pine. The trees don't move when they see a car coming. One tree doesn't warn another, "Quick, get out of the way. Here comes a SUV."

Driving drowsy is so dangerous it has been equated with drunk driving. In both conditions a person's judgment is impaired. So is reaction time and coordination. The country of New Jersey has a law that a person can be ticketed for "driving while drowsy." I'm not sure how they enforce it. Maybe a person yawns while getting a traffic ticket. Maybe a person can't stay awake while handing over the license and registration. Maybe a person nods off while reaching for the insurance card.

Sleep deprivation has been associated with obesity. There is a negative correlation between hours of sleep and the risk of being obese. The fewer hours of sleep, the greater the risk of being overweight. People who averaged less than four hours sleep were 73% more likely to be obese. People who averaged five hours had a 50% risk. People who averaged six hours had a 23% risk. The database consisted of eighteen thousand participants in a Federal survey. Variables such as exercise and overall health were accounted for in the study.

The risk of obesity may derive from the simple fact that being awake allows more time to eat. The couch potatoes extend their hours far into the night. The risk may also derive from a biological cause, as sleep deprivation reduces the level of leptin, a hormone that suppresses appetite.

The loss of sleep may interfere with the formation of memories. It is believed that REM sleep plays a role in the consolidation of memories. This may be a reason why babies and children have more REM sleep than adults—they are consolidating more memories than older people.

The experimental procedure that studies REM deprivation and memory consolidation is simplicity itself. Participants memorize a list of words or a complex story before retiring to a sleep laboratory. This happens one participant at a time, it goes without saying. Members of the experimental group are woken up whenever they enter REM sleep. They are not allowed any REM. (On returning to sleep, we enter NREM sleep.) Members of one control group are woken up the same number of times in NREM sleep as the experimental group was woken up. Members of a second control group are allowed to sleep the night through. The following morning, on awakening, all participants are asked to recollect as many words or details of the story as possible. Participants in the REM-sleep deprived experimental group performed poorest and retrieved the fewest items. Participants who slept the entire night retrieved the most items. Participants woken up in various stages of NREM sleep retrieved an intermediate number of items.

There's an important study tip in this research. Many students say they study, but they do poorly on the quiz. Probably, they crammed the night before the quiz. It may be they did not get enough sleep. They come in and take the quiz while in a groggy state. They come in and take the quiz without sufficient REM consolidation of the material. It is imperative that students get a solid night's sleep before the quiz. To do otherwise is to sabotage oneself.

Sleep deprivation may interfere with creativity. The experimental procedure is similar to that of memory research. In this case participants were architecture students. The night before they go to sleep in a sleep laboratory they were given a surprise assignment—design a particular type of building. Participants in the experimental group were woken up whenever they entered REM sleep. They were not allowed any REM. Participants in one control group were woken up the same number of times in NREM sleep as members of the experimental group were woken up. Participants in a second control group were allowed to sleep the entire night. The following morning participants in all three groups present a draft of the project. Instructors rated the drafts without knowing which group the students were in. The drafts handed in by the experimental group were judged to be less creative than the drafts from the other two groups.

The message is clear. If we want the streams of creativity to flow unimpeded, we need to get a good night's sleep. This accords with folk wisdom. We may have found an old wives' tale that's true. Creative people say when the juice of creativity gets jammed, as in writer's block, or in artist's block or in musician's block, they "sleep on" the problem. They wake up properly refreshed and they find the solution. They know how the plot progresses. They know what pastels to use. They know how to complete the lyric.

I'll like to mention a last effect of sleep deprivation. It may be that lack of sleep increases fear and a negative outlook. In this study members of the experimental group were kept up for thirty-five hours. They were then shown pictures that ranged from innocuous scenes to gruesome images of corpses and bloodshed. Activity in the amygdala, an organ of the brain involved with fear and with strong emotion, was monitored as the participants watched these images. Members of a control group who were not sleep deprived saw the same images while their amygdalas were monitored. Results showed an increase in amygdala activity in the experimental group relative to the control group. The study suggests that sleep deprivation may intensify fear and negative emotions. The world becomes a frightening place to people who do not get sufficient sleep.

These lines of research suggest we pay a serious, even deadly, price if we do not get sufficient sleep. Without sufficient sleep we make mistakes. We forget things. We can't come up with creative solutions. We are afraid and we see the world as a frightening place. This past New Year's I took relatives for a ride on the Staten Island ferry. While waiting for the ferry we watched electronic advertisements whiz by over the doors at the Whitehall St. terminal. One sign read, "Sleep deprivation affects the bottom line." This statement is true behind the steering wheel of a car barreling beyond the posted speed. It's true in college classrooms. It's true in corporate boardrooms. Sometimes there's truth in advertising.

This statement is also true in grammar schools and high schools. Parents must be careful that their children get the right amount of sleep. Grade-school children should get ten hours sleep a night. Let me repeat—grade-school children should get ten hours sleep a night. Teenagers should get nine hours sleep a night. Let me try to keep a straight face and repeat that—teenagers should get nine hours sleep a night.

Parents know how difficult it is to get their children to sleep. There are so many electronic distractions. In one survey only 20% of teens reported sleeping nine hours. Fifty percent slept less than eight hours. A quarter of the respondents reported that they fell asleep in class on occasion.

These late night interactions with electronic gadgets can lead to impaired concentration, irritability, tiredness, attention deficiencies, and to lowered grades.

Grade-school children who have television sets in their bedrooms lose an average of half an hour sleep a night. This is two-and-a-half hours of sleep debt a week. The effect is, like I said, impaired concentration, irritability, tiredness, attention deficiencies, and lowered grades.

What can parents do? Parents can banish the television set from the bedroom—even with the volume turned off, the machines are glowing in radiant splendor. If the children won't allow that, parents can enforce a "quiet time" when the televisions and computers and cell phones are turned off a half hour before bed. This quiet time can include reading and conversation. And parents can eliminate drinks like soda and coffee. These drinks contain caffeine and may be stimulating the children at the worst possible time.

In our ways we're all children at heart. This advice to parents isn't bad advice when it comes to adults. Adults need a quiet time before sleeping when we're not glued to a screen. We watch the news and hear about the murder and mayhem breaking out across the big city—and then we click the set off and go to bed. No wonder we can't sleep. No wonder we have anxiety dreams. Or we watch a R-rated movie—*Friday the Thirteenth* meets *Hellraiser*. The movie ends in gory fashion—and then we click the set off and go to bed. No wonder we can't sleep. No wonder we have anxiety dreams.

We need a quiet time before sleeping. We also need darkness. The pineal gland secretes a hormone called *melatonin*. This hormone slows bodily functions and promotes sleep. It's secreted only in darkness. Keeping brightly lit televisions and computer screens on impedes the release of melatonin. Our sleep is not as deep as it should be.

There are a number of sleep disorders. *Sleep apnea* is a condition in which a person cannot sleep and breathe at the same time. *Narcolepsy* is a disorder in which a person is overwhelmed by sleep. These two conditions require medical intervention.

The most common sleep disorder is related to lifestyle rather than to the brain. This is *insomnia*, which is defined as *a failure to fall asleep or to stay asleep*. More than a third of Americans report experiencing insomnia at some point in their lives. A third of Americans seems like an underestimate.

The single greatest cause of insomnia is *stress*. Our spouses are causing stress. Our children are causing stress. Our jobs are causing stress. It is difficult to sleep when we're assailed by worries, fears, and problems. It's difficult to fall asleep if we think something bad is going to happen or if we think our situation is growing worse.

Another prominent cause of insomnia is the use of *alcohol*. This may be the case of a problem drinker or the case of a person who uses alcohol as part of the sleep ritual. People who use alcohol have no problem falling asleep. Their problem is staying asleep. Alcohol reduces REM sleep—we know the kind of effect that can have. When it's time to enter REM, alcoholics wake up. When alcoholics go on the wagon and stop drinking they run the risk of experiencing nightmares. This is REM rebound. I suppose the moral here is don't use alcohol to induce sleep. Or if you use alcohol, don't stop.

Another cause of insomnia is the use of *sleeping pills*. These pills, which are advertised round-the-clock on television, serve a purpose—all of us encounter periodic episodes of sleeplessness. But these pills should never be used for more than a few weeks. They affect the brain chemistry in unpredictable ways and people can become dependent on them. They become part of the sleep ritual. When we stop taking them, we can't fall asleep.

To avoid and minimize the risk of insomnia look at the causes of sleeplessness. Don't use alcohol to induce sleep. Don't rely on sleeping pills for more than a few weeks. Try to get a handle on the sources of stress. If your spouse is causing stress, divorce him or her. If your children are causing stress, give them up for adoption. If your job is causing stress, quit. When you eliminate these sources of stress, you'll sleep like a baby.

Here are a few other tips to avoid insomnia. Try to set a schedule of sleeping and waking—sleep is a habit in addition to being a biological need. Go to bed only when tired. Don't do anything else in bed but sleep. Study at the kitchen table. Have sex on the living room couch. You want to reserve the bed for one thing and that's sleeping—it becomes a kind of conditioning. If you can't fall asleep within fifteen minutes, get out of bed. The personality theorist Alfred Adler told insomniac patients that staying awake provided a chance for them to think of all the good things they could do for people—his helpful advice promptly propelled them into the soundest sleep. Prof. Ford advises students who can't sleep to get out of bed and study psychology. Sometimes insomnia is a good thing. It gives students the chance to improve their grades.

The great thing about sleep is that we *dream*. As we sleep movies play in the theaters of our minds. The movies are vivid, emotional, crazy, scary, sexy, funny, and in color. We don't create dreams. We don't think them up. They come to us unbidden. And they're free. Think how much it costs to watch a movie at the local cinema. As we sleep we can watch a movie for free, a movie that is us. We're the audience, we're the actors, we're the directors, we're the stage hands, we're the writers, for all I know we may be the producers. When we study our dreams, we become the reviewers. Dreaming is like going to the eight-screen movie palace, buying a ticket, and not knowing what's going to appear on the screen.

Throughout history people have been trying to uncover the relationship of dreams to our waking lives. Some people believe that dreams are supernatural events full of mysteries and precognitive marvels. These people find support for their views in religious books. Think of the Hebrew Testament story of Joseph who interpreted Pharaoh's dreams. Think of the Christian Testament and of a different Joseph, who is told by the angel to get out of Bethlehem one mule ride ahead of Herod's henchmen. These people also find support in modern culture. Movies and books frequently portray dreams as superior to our conscious lives and as connected to ethereal sources in The Great Beyond.

Other people have a different view of dreams. For these people, dreams are big nothings. Dreams depend on what we ate before retiring—those spicy meatballs inspire dreams of fire and those bottles of Mexican beer inspire a sea voyage in stormy weather.

It's only been since the nineteenth century that people have tried to interpret dreams in a psychological sense that neither inflates them to supernatural realms nor deflates them to last night's six-course dinner. One of the first to give dreams a strictly psychological meaning was Sigmund Freud. Freud believed that dreams combined ordinary memories with the disguised expressions of repressed sexual and aggressive desires. These desires—*wishes*, he called them—couldn't appear in dreams in their naked obviousness, but they could appear in altered and symbolic form. By guiding patients to understand these images, psychoanalysts could help dissolve the repressions that seal the wishes in corked bottles in the preconscious sea.

Freud made the interpretation of dreams an important component of his psychotherapy and he believed his dream theory was his greatest accomplishment. He said of himself that he was the man who "disturbed the sleep of the world." We now know he was blowing a head of steam. Nowadays, few people believe Freud's dream theory. The few who do live on Central Park West.

We can understand dreams as *thoughts and thought processes that occur under the condition of sleep.* Paradoxical sleep dreams are vivid, emotional, bizarre, and irrational. They don't correspond with reality, perhaps because paradoxical sleep is an unusual experience in which the brain is fully active and alert and the body is unresponsive. The "unusual experience" is both for the brain and for the dreamer—we note here, as in the lecture on the brain, the strange bifurcation between our selves and our brains. "Run!" the brain commands and the legs don't comply. "Hit back!" the brain commands and the hands don't form fists. "Shout for help!" the brain commands and the lips don't purse. The brain commands and there's no compliance and no feedback. I imagine the brain must be mighty perplexed.

Quiet sleep dreams are less vivid, less bizarre, less emotional, and more rational. They roughly correspond with ordinary thinking. They make more sense and are more directly reflective of reality. This may lie in the correspondence of brain and bodily feedback.

The relationship of dreams to waking life is quite direct. Whatever we experience in our daily lives will turn up in our dreams. Whatever concerns us in our waking lives will concern us in our dreams. Whatever we think about while awake, we will think about in our sleep—it will come to us on the big screen. Granted, paradoxical sleep dreams show us these thoughts in strange and weird ways. Quiet sleep shows us these thoughts in more direct and ordinary ways.

The content of dreams reflects who we are. They are not different than we are. There is no separate self, no psychic double or secret personality. Sexually active people have dreams of sex. Repressed and prudish people have repressed and prudish dreams. Religious people have dreams with religious images. Materialists have dreams, I don't know, about dollar bills and cash registers. Aggressive people have dreams full of aggression. Timid people have tranquil dreams—maybe they have anxiety dreams. Creative people have interesting dreams. Non-creative people have dull dreams. If people have psychic powers in their waking lives, their dreams will be full of supernatural occurrences. If people lack psychic powers awake, they won't be visited by paranormal entities and their sleep will be uneventful.

In terms of some of the percentages, 95% of people report that they dream. More than two-thirds report they have recurring dreams. Surprisingly, 40% report that they can control their dreams while they're in them—this is called *lucid dreaming* and it sounds intriguing. Most dreams do not contain sexual images—about one in ten dreams for men and one in thirty dreams for women. More women than men report dreams of being chased and more women than men report dreams of being attacked. Dreams of falling are experienced at the same percentages by both men and women.

Both genders report dreams of frustration, such as trying to do something and failing. Interestingly, more women than men report seeing a dead person as alive in dreams and of seeing a living person as dead. Perhaps the latter is a wish.

Freud conjectured that we fail to remember dreams because they show us things about ourselves we prefer not to know and try to repress or suppress. This conjecture sounds like it might be true—I know I prefer upbeat movies about myself in the theater of the mind. But the reason we fail to remember dreams may be less exotic than Freud suggested—the reason involves *retroactive interference*. As you remember from the memory lecture, retroactive interference is the situation in which new memories interfere with the retrieval of old memories. Memories of the tasks ahead of us during the day interfere with the memory of last night's dream.

We have an impressive dream, a dream we want to remember. But as soon as we wake up, the daylight world crashes on us like a mudslide of memories and plans. We're late for work. We have to prepare our notes. We have to check our funds. We have to make breakfast. We have to get the kids off to school. We have to walk the dog. Now what was that dream, that impressive dream, that dream we wanted to recollect? Of course, it's gone into oblivion. It never got into long-term memory. The first few REM dreams never got in long-term memory because we stayed asleep and didn't rehearse them. The last one had the chance, but newer thoughts and memories sent it reeling.

We might want to disregard the first few REM dreams—we certainly don't want to stay up all night fussing with dreams. If we want to keep the last REM dream of the night from entering oblivion, we need to keep retroactive interference from occurring. This isn't difficult to do.

When you wake up, don't move. Don't move a muscle. Lie there and let the dream coalesce. The dream is like spume from the bubbling stream of unconsciousness. When you are sure the dream won't evaporate in the morning sun of consciousness, get out of bed and write an outline of the dream. You needn't write the entire dream, as it can be long and complicated and you don't want to be late for class. You can write a few key words—school, straws, academic deans, Komodo dragons. Remember what we suggested in the memory lecture—by writing the dream down, you make it permanent. You can then go about your daily tasks confident that you won't forget the dream.

Alternately, you can buy a voice-activated recorder and recite your dream, but be sure no one is in earshot. Events in dreams can sometimes be a tad embarrassing.

Once your dream is on paper and permanent, you can carry it around with you. You can think about the dream throughout the day. You can even tell it to someone, if you're so inclined. When you have time, you can write the dream in full in a dream diary. What you'll find as you keep a dream diary is that certain themes and events and places and characters repeat themselves. There's nothing mysterious or supernatural about this. Don't worry, you're not slipping into "the other place." You're discovering the person you are—very likely, you knew this person beforehand. The themes—the story lines of the movies in our sleep—concern our personalities and the issues we face on a daily basis. We're constantly meeting ourselves in our dreams, which may or may not be a pleasant experience.

Should you buy a dictionary of dream symbols? You can, if you want to waste ten dollars plus tax. The images in our dreams—roses and boats and knives and Komodo dragons, to name four—are unique, because they refer to our personalities and to the issues we face. Sure, there are broad personality types and, sure, there are issues faced by everyone, but there are always going to be differences among people and it's the differences that are crucial.

Consider the symbol of a rose. It will mean one thing to a person who's fallen in love. It'll mean something different to a guy who's fallen in love with a lady named Rose. It'll mean something different to a guy trying to make up with a different lady named Rose. It'll mean something different to a florist. It'll mean something different to a landscaper. It'll mean something different to a botanist. It'll mean something different to a person who's been at a bridal shower. It'll mean something different to a person who's been at a funeral. Each symbol has unique connotations that can't be captured in dictionaries.

In conclusion, I wish you all get solid sleep, keep your sleep debt under the interest rate of good health, and have pleasant dreams.

Thank you.

TIPS TO STUDENTS ~
The Use of Study Cards

Frequently, quizzes require students to match one item of information with another item of information. For example, when students see "Delta brain waves," this phrase should connect to, "How NREM sleep is assessed."

A good system for this kind of connecting or associating one item of information with another is the use of a set of study cards. Study cards are usually index cards that contain a key word on one side and the information that the key word is associated with on the other side. So, "Delta brain waves" is written on one side of the card and "How NREM sleep is assessed" is written on the other side.

Here are some tips with the use of study cards.

If the textbook has a set of key words or definitions at the end of each chapter, write each word on one side of a card and a brief definition or example on the other side.

If the textbook does not have key words or definitions at the end of each chapter, you can impose an organization of your own. Often, important concepts in chapters are in boldface or in italics. These are the words you'd want to place on study cards.

You should carry the cards as you travel to and from school and work. (They're much lighter than the textbook.) Test yourself frequently. Look at the key word and try to think of the definition. Don't force yourself to retrieve the answer. If you can't retrieve the answer promptly, turn the card over and read the definition.

You should shuffle the cards every so often, so you do not learn the information in a specific order.

If you notice that you have trouble with a particular key word or with a particular topic, you can set those cards aside and spend extra study time with them and with the section of the textbook they derive from.

You can slowly remove cards as you become proficient with the information and replace these cards with new key words.

Lecture Two ~
Motivation

I'll like to start the lecture on motivation by inviting you to close your eyes and think. Think about anything you want. Some of you may well be thinking, "This is an odd exercise." Some may be thinking, "Will I get credit for thinking?" Some unlucky few may be rehearsing grievances and think about the ills done to them in the past. The majority are probably thinking about something they're going to do later. Maybe it's a household chore. Maybe it's an errand. Maybe it's a class assignment. Maybe it's a place you want to go. Maybe it's a person you want to meet.

My point in asking you to close your eyes and think is to suggest that we always seem to be living a little in the future. As the saying goes, "We understand our lives looking backward and we live our lives looking forward." I think Soren Kierkegaard said this—it may have been the guy who hung out at the bus station. We are always motivated to go forward to where we hope to be. Sometimes we are motivated to go forward to avoid the place we currently inhabit.

I have three topics to cover in the lecture on motivation. I'll like to review the different interpretations and theories about motivation. Then I'll like to consider hunger and eating as a typical motive. And I'll like to consider what happens when a motive goes awry—in this case when eating becomes disconnected from hunger.

Motivation can be defined as *the study of the hypothetical states within an organism that activate and direct behavior.*

Some of these states are going to be physiological. Others will be psychological. Others will be an amalgam of physiology and psychology. Some of these states propel us toward people and things. We are said to approach stimuli. Some of these states propel us in the opposite direction away from people and things. We are said to avoid stimuli. And we may find that certain people or things are pulling us toward them.

Motivation studies what gets us off the couch and into motion. Sometimes it's just to move from the living room into the kitchen to grab a bowl of snacks. Sometimes it's to move across vast distances, as when we are motivated to pursue a college degree or when we plan a wedding or engage in a creative endeavor. Motivation studies what gets us moving the minute it takes to go into the kitchen. And motivation studies what keeps us moving on the same task across the years.

Motivation also studies how our movements come to be directed. As we grow up and experience life, we come to be directed or channeled in our thoughts and behaviors. We don't move willy-nilly. We move toward and away from specific goals. We don't go to the bookstore and say, "Mister Bookseller, give me any book you like reading." No, we go to our favorite section and find our favorite author. And we don't go to the delicatessen and say, "Mister Deli-man, build me any twelve-inch sandwich on any kind of bread you like slicing." No, we order our sandwich the way we want it down to the savory level of the condiments. And we don't go to the tavern and say, "Mr. Barkeep, give me any drink you feel like pouring." No, we order our favorite beverage and it better come the way we like it.

The history of the topic of motivation began in the late nineteenth century with the study of *instincts*. As you can guess, instinct theories were given special impetus by Darwin's views on natural selection.

An instinct—the up-to-date term is *fixed action pattern*—is an *inherited biological disposition to respond in an exact way to a specific stimulus*. Instincts are species specific. That is, all members of a species respond to the stimulus in the same way and show the same behaviors.

Specifically, a *releasing stimulus* elicits a *fixed* (or *modal*) *action pattern*. Neither the stimulus nor the behavior is learned. They are part of the organism's endowment as a member of a particular species.

To some extent, the behavior is modifiable by experience and it is modifiable by changes in the releasing stimulus.

When I was a child I was into tropical fish. It was a time-consuming and expensive hobby. All the fish I bought died soon after the purchase. Maybe the temperature of the water was too cool. Maybe the temperature was too warm. Maybe the water wasn't fully oxygenated. Maybe it was overly oxygenated. I don't know why the fish died. They just died and I was out a lot of allowance money.

There is a species of tropical fish called the Siamese Fighting Fish. Males have long gaudy fins that are brightly colored. Females are drab looking—they can't help it. The females don't appear to be worth fighting over, but I don't see them in the way the male fish do. Customers are told never to put two males in the same tank. The people who say this know what they are talking about. The gaudy fins serve as releasing stimuli and elicit aggression. If one male sees the fins of another male, it attacks. We can cut and paint a wood figure of the fish and drop it in the tank. The male will attack the wood. We can put a mirror in the tank and the male will attack its own reflection. Of course, it's a fish and it doesn't know who it is.

Siamese Fighting Fish are born knowing how to act and what to attack. They don't learn this behavior in school. Their parents don't teach them. Their older brothers don't tell them. Their girlfriends don't urge them to fight. They know what to do ahead of time because that's how God and Darwin built their species.

Consider the behavior of birds. The parent bird catches and eats an insect and returns to the nest. The size, shape, and coloration of the parent's beak serve as a releasing stimulus for the baby bird. As soon as the baby bird sees the beak, it starts to peck. The pecking, in turn, causes the parent bird to regurgitate the insect, which serves as breakfast, lunch, or dinner, as the case might be. This sounds pretty disgusting. Personally, I think this is the reason birds never advanced as a species.

I mentioned that the fixed action pattern is modifiable. This can be seen in the bird example. Let's say the releasing stimulus is a yellow beak with a central red dot. Experiments can change the coloration of the beak—it can even be a fake beak. Changing the coloration changes the rate of pecking in the baby bird. Intensify the red dot and the rate of pecking increases. Wash the red out and the pecking decreases.

Instinct theories of motivation were popular in the early part of the twentieth century, but they were replaced in America by behaviorism. What happened is that people started to look for human characteristics in animals. They still do. And long lists of human instincts were drawn up. Everything people did was called "instinctual." If I acted friendly, I expressed the instinct for friendship. If I acted aggressively, I expressed the instinct for aggressiveness. If I liked to buy things, I expressed the instinct of acquisitiveness. If I liked to give things away, I expressed the instinct of generosity. And so on and on.

Everything we did was called an instinct. Calling behavior "instinctual" really added little to the study of behavior. The concept of instinct became vaporous. The vast role of learning was overlooked. So was the notion of a specific releasing stimulus. Anything could trigger friendliness. Anything could trigger aggressiveness. Anything could trigger acquisitiveness—handbags do this to a lady I know. Anything could trigger generosity. This huge—human—medley of stimuli was far removed from specific releasing stimuli like gaudy fins in male Siamese Fighting Fish and red dots on yellow beaks in birds.

A more sophisticated form of instinct theory was developed later in the twentieth century in Europe. It was developed by a number of famous scientists including Konrad Lorenz, Niko Tinbergen, and Karl von Fritsch. Lorenz was famous for his work on *imprinting*. This is a species-specific behavior pattern seen in waterfowl. These birds are programmed by God and Darwin to follow a moving object they see a few hours after birth. The usual moving object is the mother goose. Some of us have sat in traffic waiting for the procession of the mother goose and her chicks to cross the road. If you come upon such a procession, be patient and don't do anything rash. In most states it's a crime to harm these birds. To get back to imprinting, some unlucky geese imprint on the wrong moving object, like a dog or cat, even on a human being. There are movies of Mother Lorenz being followed by a gaggle of geese.

In the United States instinct theory was replaced by behavioral and physiological theories. These theories initially had a reductionistic and steady state orientation. The idea is that we are motivated to keep stimulation and arousal as low as possible. You might remember the views of Sigmund Freud, who viewed pleasure as the reduction of stimulation.

Psychoanalysis can be construed as a theory of motivation—and of what can go wrong with the motives of sex and aggression.

Walter Cannon (1871-1945) was a prominent physiologist and best-selling author—one of his books was entitled *The Wisdom of the Body*. Cannon popularized an important concept called *homeostasis*. Homeostasis is *the tendency of the body to keep a steady state and to avoid extremes*. We can observe homeostasis in the control of body temperature. If the blood cools, we shiver to get the temperature back up. If the blood warms, we sweat to lower the temperature. We can also observe homeostasis in the relationship of glucose and insulin. As glucose increases, the body secretes insulin to lower glucose. And as insulin increases, the body is motivated to increase the level of glucose.

Clark Hull (1884-1952) was an important learning psychologist. Like Freud and Cannon, Hull favored a reductionistic view of motivation. Hull advanced the concept of *drive*, which is an aroused physiological state. This is not necessarily sexual arousal, but a state of generalized arousal and activity based on physiological needs. Think how we feel and act when we're hungry or thirsty or in pain. Think how we feel when we're filled with irreversible lust—maybe we don't want to think about that.

Hull postulated that reinforcement occurs when a drive is reduced. Think how you satisfy hunger or thirst or pain or lust. You probably repeat the same behavior that worked the previous time. This concept may explain the directionality of motives. We tend to return to our favorite snack or drink or pain medication or naughty practice. We do so because these behaviors reduced or eliminated drives in the past.

Hull suggested that reinforcement works through the reduction of drives. Later psychologists suggested that Hull had the thermos half filled. Yes, it is reinforcing to reduce arousal. But the absence of arousal can be aversive. It can be reinforcing to increase arousal.

We find it aversive when arousal is too high, but think of the opposite case. Think what happens when we get sick or get stuck indoors for too long. We say we are "bored to death" or that we suffer from "cabin fever." We go out of our way to become active and "make things happen." We "shake things up" and "break loose" and "break out" because it is aversive to be unaroused and inactive for too long.

So it's reinforcing to reduce arousal when it gets too high. And it's reinforcing to increase arousal when it gets too low. There are individual differences in terms of what levels of arousal are tolerated. Some people can handle high arousal with aplomb and some people can't. Some people can handle inactivity well and others can't. There is a trait of personality related to how people handle low arousal and inactivity. The trait is called *sensation-seeking*. People who score high on surveys assessing this trait are thrill seekers. They like adventure. They go on roller coasters. They parachute. They surf. They hunt big game on safaris. They can't stay still for extended periods. They hate boredom. They hate inactivity. They hate low arousal.

In mid-twentieth century America motivation became subservient to the learning concepts of reinforcement and punishment. People become motivated to do what earns them reinforcement. People become motivated to avoid what earns them punishment. Reinforcement and punishment were construed to be the blades that sliced our personalities, firming up and defining some aspects of our lives and snipping off other aspects. If we received reinforcement we were psychologically sculpt into buff specimens, like Michelangelo's *David*. If we received punishment we finished like those limbless and headless statues found in Roman excavations.

Later in the century a controversial psychologist named Richard Herrnstein advanced the concept of the *matching law*. Herrstein was controversial for co-authoring a book called *The Bell Curve* that suggested that there were racial differences in intelligence. He died soon after the book was published, leaving his co-author to bear the brunt of criticism.

The matching law states that there is a *positive correlation between the rate of response and the number of reinforcements a person received*. We do what we have been most often reinforced for doing. We do most often what we have been most often reinforced for doing. Given a choice, we prefer to do what we have been most often reinforced for doing.

The matching law is solid behaviorism because it explains choice and decision making without recourse to cognitive concepts or to personality. Consider a not uncommon experience. Parents say their high school son is good in sports but a "lazy student." Parents look to the personality of their son and to the trait of laziness. The matching law suggests they should be looking to something different than personality traits. The choice of playing sports or studying follows the matching law and has nothing to do with personality. Given a choice, the boy does what he has been most often reinforced for doing—in this case, for playing sports. The boy gets a lot of reinforcement for playing sports. The reinforcement is immediate—the coach praises him, his teammates jump on him, the crowd in the stands erupts with applause. He doesn't get a lot of reinforcement for studying. He may even be punished for studying. He may get low grades and he may be nagged and vexed by concerned parents. Who would choose to study for a test when he can hear the coach's approbation? Who would choose to sit in libraries when he can get the high fives of teammates? Who would choose to be nagged to no end by high-achievement parents when he can hear the approving screams of the fans?

Psychologists also tweaked the idea of reinforcement and punishment by adding another wrinkle in the stretchable fabric of learning. It may be that *some people prefer to receive reinforcement even at the risk of getting punished.* And it be may be *other people prefer to avoid punishment even at the risk of losing reinforcement.*

Some people put their feet to the pedal to make the green light before it changes to yellow. These people speed regardless of the risk of getting a traffic ticket or worse. Some people rush and introduce themselves to the prettiest or most handsome person in the club. These people risk getting clobbered by the person's date. And some people like to play for high stakes at the blackjack table in the Borgata casino.

You may be like that kind of person and God bless you. Or you may be like my kind of person and prefer to avoid punishment. Sure, I want reinforcements and plenty of them. But I also want to live safely and wisely. I don't want to get in trouble. The traffic light is green, but I slow down. I don't want to get a ticket. I don't want to get into an accident. I'm sure the light is going to change to red before I arrive at the intersection. Sure, I want to associate with good-looking people. But I don't want to be rejected. I don't want to be punched in the nose by a jealous boyfriend. Sure, I want to hit it big in the casino. But I'll probably lose the fifty dollars I bring on my next excursion to Atlantic City.

As with all traits, most individuals score in the average range on surveys on these preferences. Extreme scores are rare, but they occur. When extreme scores occur in the preference to obtain reinforcement a person's behavior may be said to become *impulsive*. You've seen enough movies where the character bets everything on a single card. This happens infrequently in real life. When extreme scores occur in the preference to avoid punishment a person's behavior may be said to become *anxious*. I'm sure you've seen enough movies about wallflowers wandering the fringes of the dancehall. This happens all too frequently in real life.

Psychologists have also tweaked the concept of reinforcement by focusing on the concepts of *extrinsic reinforcement* and *intrinsic reinforcement*.

Some people are governed by extrinsic reinforcement. They are *motivated to perform for money or for recognition or for fame* and for what Carl Gustav Jung called "profit and honor." A chef cooks because he gets paid for it—if he's lucky, he'll get a program on the food network. And an author writes to sell her stories—if she's lucky, she'll make the bestseller charts. Other people are governed by intrinsic reinforcement. They are *motivated to perform for the sheer love and joy a behavior brings them*. A chef may prepare meals, but only in his home and for his family. He loves to cook, he doesn't care about getting on television. And a writer may write for the sheer delight in putting her thoughts on paper. She loves to write, she doesn't care about publishing a bestseller. In this regard I'll like to point out that there are many people who keep journals and diaries. You have only to visit a Barnes & Noble superstore to see how many blank journals are for sale.

What's interesting is when one type of reinforcement shifts to the other type. Think of a person who is governed by extrinsic reinforcement. The chef is fired. Does he want to prepare gourmet meals for free? No one wants to publish the writer. Does she stay at home stringing sentences together for no pay?

And think of the situation where people who were governed by intrinsic reinforcement start to receive recognition or pay for their work. This sounds like an ideal situation. The chef becomes a household name. The writer makes the charts. But it may not be as ideal as at first sight. The chef is now a hireling. He has a manager. He has critics who rate his food. He has picky customers who return his food. The writer is now famous. But she has an editor. She has critics. She is now under contract and has to produce masterpiece after masterpiece where before she could let the Muse come and go at leisure. Doing something for the sheer joy and love is quite a different scenario than getting paid to do it. Doing something for the sheer joy and love is quite a different scenario than doing it under the guidance of managers and critics and customers.

The social psychologist Philip Zimbardo tells a funny story about what can happen when intrinsic reinforcement changes into extrinsic reinforcement. (We'll encounter Zimbardo again in the lecture on social psychology.) Zimbardo grew up in a place called Brooklyn—maybe you heard of it. There are a lot of tough young men in Brooklyn or so they keep telling everyone. Zimbardo was not one of them. The local bully—let's call him "Ralph"—loved to pick on Philip. It was sheer joy and delight to knock Philip around. One day Philip got the idea to put psychology into action. Right before Ralph was going to hit him, Philip said, "Wait. I'll give you fifty cents to hit me." Ralph was stunned, but he took the fifty cents and hit Philip. This went on for a while. Ralph came around one day ready to get his fifty cents and Philip said he didn't have fifty cents. He had only a quarter—he told Ralph his allowance had been cut. Ralph was annoyed, but he took the quarter and hit Philip. This went on for a while. One day, just as he was about to get hit, Philip announced he didn't have any money. Ralph could hit him for free, if he wanted to. Ralph had no part of that. There was no way Ralph was going to hit Philip without getting paid to do it.

Zimbardo's story has relevance for parents and for educators who get the idea to pay students for doing homework and for attending class. Unless the motivation to study and to attend class becomes intrinsic, the students will perform only as long as the extrinsic reinforcer—the money—is forthcoming. Take away the money and the behavior will likely cease.

There's a last concept that derives from learning psychology that I'll like to mention. This is the concept of *incentives*, which are *inherently valuable or desirable qualities of particular reinforcers*. If I may be politically incorrect, not all reinforcers are created equal. Some reinforcers possess qualities that, for whatever reason, make them desirable. There's a Big Mac. There's a flank cut of Delmonico steak. There's Easy Jesus brandy. There's Remy Martin X/O brandy. There's the homely girl at the check out counter in the Dollar General. There's the glamorous girl who's smiling at me in the cologne aisle in Macy's. There's a fig newton. And there's a chocolate raspberry linzer bar.

Many years ago the bakery in Macy's Cellar sold chocolate raspberry linzer bars. I use to take the train from Chambers St. to Herald Square to buy them by the box load. If the train wasn't running, I'd walk. I can still see the pastry. I can still taste it—two inches of chocolate and one inch of raspberry. The dough was made the Austrian way with almonds ground up in it. They don't serve chocolate raspberry linzer bars on the ferry to The Great Beyond.

Anyway, back to an off-brand reality that contains fig newtons. Our behavior and our motivation can be controlled by incentives. We are motivated to get and to keep reinforcements of intrinsically high quality. I wouldn't walk from Chambers St. to Herald Square to buy a box of fig newtons. I wouldn't even take the train.

In the 1940s colleagues of Clark Hull demonstrated how strongly incentives control behavior. One experiment was done by a researcher named Crespi. He was called "The Amazing Crespi," but only behind his back.

The experiments involved shifting reinforcements after learning took place. One group of rats learned to run a maze—this is one rat at a time. At the end of the maze they found a high incentive food that served as reinforcement. The food was bran mash, which is the rat equivalent of linzer cookies. This group learned the maze quickly. They made few mistakes. A second group of rats learned to run the same maze. At the end of the maze they found a low incentive food that served as reinforcement. This was sunflower seeds, which is the rat equivalent of fig newtons. This group took longer to learn the maze than the first group and they made more mistakes.

At this point in the experiment Crespi reversed the reinforcements. The group that received bran mash found sunflower seeds at the end of the maze. They must have been surprised and disappointed. The group that received sunflower seeds found bran mash at the end of the maze. They must have been surprised and delighted.

The shift in reinforcement caused a shift in the behavior of the groups. The group that had received sunflower seeds as a reinforcer and suddenly found bran mash started to speed up and to make fewer mistakes. Their behavior improved. The group that had received bran mash as a reinforcer and suddenly found sunflower seeds slowed down and started to make mistakes. Their behavior deteriorated. In fact, this group ran slower and made more mistakes than a control group that received sunflower seeds throughout the experiment.

Note how the behavior of the rats corresponded to the nature of the reinforcement. And note how changing the nature of the reinforcer changed the performance of the rats. There's an expression "The tail wags the dog." Here the tail of reinforcement wagged the behavior of the rat. I ask you to consider how you would respond if your pay shifted. You were making $50,000 annually. Now you're making $25,000 annually. I think you'd lose your motivation. You'd slow down. You'd make mistakes. You wouldn't care about losing a low-paying job after you had a high-paying job. And consider the reverse. You were making $25,000 annually. Now you're making $50,000 annually. I think your motivation would improve. You'd speed up. You'd be careful to avoid making mistakes. You'd care very much about losing a high-paying job after you had a low-paying job.

We started the survey of the concept of motivation with instinct theory. Then we reviewed how in America motivation became enmeshed with the concepts of homeostasis and learning—this wasn't necessarily true in Europe, but who cares about Europe? The last stop in this survey is how motivation was construed in the tradition of humanistic psychology.

Humanistic psychology was a diverse movement within many subfields of psychology that commenced in the 1960s. It was tied in with the "cultural revolutions" of those years. And it was tied in with the counter-culture and with the upheavals of young people against the suffocating hypocrisies of the previous generations. Much of humanistic psychology was faddish and ephemeral. With a few exceptions, it has faded. One of those exceptions has to do with motivation.

One of the founders of humanistic psychology was Carl Rogers (1902-1987), who developed a highly influential type of psychotherapy called "person-centered therapy." Another founder was Abraham Maslow (1908-1970), who developed a concept within motivation called the *hierarchy of needs*. This concept is one element of humanistic psychology that has endured. In fact, it has become widely popular in business, management, and human resources.

Maslow was born in a place called Brooklyn. He died in California. I imagine everyone born in Brooklyn wants to die in California. When

I found out Maslow was from Brooklyn I wrote then Mayor Koch that New York ought to name a street or one of those little parks at intersections after Maslow. I wasn't asking for an avenue. I wasn't asking to rename the borough of Brooklyn "Maslow." All I asked for was one block—it could have been a dead end. After all, Maslow was about the most famous psychologist to come out of Brooklyn. Unfortunately, I never received a reply. Never receiving replies is the story of my life.

Maslow believed psychology gave students the wrong *image of humanity*. If not the wrong image, then an inadequate image. The Freudians implied that human beings were uncivilized lust-crazed neurotics. Trait psychologists implied that the majority of human beings could be packed in the "average" region of the normal distribution curve. Behaviorists implied that humans could be manipulated by the same conditioning procedures that tamed rats, cats and dogs. Maslow wanted to impart a more favorable, benevolent, and presumably accurate, image of people.

Freudians based their psychology on abnormal individuals. Trait psychologists based their psychology on the average individual. Usually, this individual was a college student. Behaviorists based their psychology on rats, cats and dogs. Maslow wanted to base psychology on the most intelligent, creative, and accomplished individuals—but enough about me. Let's get back to Maslow. He wanted to study the best and the brightest and the people who had achieved their lives' goals.

Maslow suggested that there are five levels in the hierarchy of needs. The levels are rather famous. Everyone's heard of them except for the people who haven't. The first level includes the *basic needs*. This level consists of satisfying the needs for food, water, and temperature control. Let's not forget the need for oxygen, although we often do. We find out just how basic the need for oxygen is the moment we don't get any.

The second level is the need for a *safe and a secure environment*. We want the world to be an orderly place. We want it to be safe and reliable. We want consistency. We want things to be where we put them. We want to meet the same people. We don't want to have to relearn things. We don't want change—not too much change, anyway. We want people and events to be predictable.

The third level includes the *belonging needs*—these are the needs for friends, for confidants, and for lovers. Human beings are social creatures through and through. We want to be with others, we want to be included. Ostracism is an ugly word for an ugly fate. Ostracism means to be left out and not to be included. Maybe that happened to you when you were a kid and your peers were choosing sides in a basketball game. Everyone gets picked but you. You have to stand on the sidelines and watch. You know how badly that felt. And maybe that happens on the job. Your co-workers go to lunch and they don't invite you. You have to eat alone. The lunchroom can be a lonely place when you're by yourself. Ostracism is a horrible experience.

The fourth level of the hierarchy includes the needs for *achievement and for recognition*. We want to be on the team—and we want to be on the starting team. We want to be one of the players—and we want to be a captain. We want to be on the yearbook staff—and we want to be editor. We want to be a clerk in the corporation—and we want to be manager. Assistant manager, anyway, since that's better than being a clerk.

The fifth and final level is the need for *self-actualization*. We want to do everything that God and Darwin put us on this earth to accomplish. We want to express all our capabilities. We want to express all our gifts. We want to express that special uniqueness that defines us more than the previous needs. We want to be all that we can be—and to do this without joining the military.

I understand self-actualization sounds mysterious. It does to me. I suppose I have no special gifts to actualize. There was a man who lived on the Lower East Side who claimed that he knew what self-actualization was. Unfortunately for everyone, he moved and didn't leave a forwarding address, so we're rather in the lurch.

Here's how I try to understand self-actualization. When I was young there was a kid in our neighborhood with superlative athletic ability. His name was Steve. I'm not going to tell you his last name in case you know him. Steve was a left-handed pitcher. He was so good we thought he was going to turn professional. Unfortunately, he never did. I ran into Steve some years later. If they weren't in my head, I wouldn't have believed my eyes. Steve was a physical wreck. He was heavy and out of shape. I was in better shape, which demonstrates the deplorable shape Steve was in. The point I'm trying to make is Steve never developed his great talent. He never self-actualized.

Let me give another example. I once met an elderly lady who was my second cousin on the paternal line. She told me her family history.

She said her father had many regrets in his old age. He came from a family of artists, but he never did any painting or drawing. He had to do that disagreeable chore most of us have to do—he had to work for a living. And hard work he did, too, on the docks of New York as a longshoreman. He never had time to express the artistic talent he was born with. Anyone with muscles and a grappling hook can be a longshoreman. Not everyone can paint and draw with talent. Her father never actualized that aspect of his personality.

Maslow suggested the hierarchy of needs corresponds with human development. Basic needs and security needs are relevant in infancy and in childhood. Babies are completely dependent on other people. Parents have to create the predictability that nourishes children. The belonging needs become relevant in the teenage and young adult years. These are the years of close friendships and of sexual friendships. Slowly, the idea of "starting a family" becomes important. Teenagers and young adults are "joiners." They want to be included in social activities. These social activities can involve the military. The government utilizes the need to belong in creating cohesive "bands of brothers." These social needs also occur in the ivy halls of academia. Think of all the teams and clubs in high school that students can join. And think of the number of clubs and fraternities and sororities that exist on college campuses. There are more than sixty on this campus.

When I was in high school I was on the yearbook staff. I was also on the varsity archery team. This was before my eyes went bad. I remember those days fondly. We use to put an apple on Mr. Albano's head—he was the archery coach—and shoot it off at fifty yards. We rarely missed.

As we mature and settle down, we advance in our chosen careers. And we feel the need for recognition. We feel the need to be acknowledged and to advance in rank. We want to get out of the cubicle and into an office, preferably a corner office. We want to get out of the mailroom and into the boardroom.

Finally, in middle age after our family has taken care of us and provided a safe secure home, and after we've found true love and raised a family, and after we've made the world safe for democracy, and after we've climbed the corporate ladder to become chairperson of the executive committee, we can retire with a golden parachute and devote ourselves to the tasks God and Darwin placed us on earth to accomplish. In a developmental sense self-actualization expresses an ancient Hindu concept. Only after we have contributed to the community as a soldier, merchant, and family man, can we retire to the ashram and find Nirvana—or whatever it is we're looking for. It may be something more modest than everlasting enlightenment.

I presented the needs in a developmental context, but we must understand that none of the needs are permanently achieved once and for good. If you choke tonight on a beer pretzel while watching the mighty *Yankees* trounce the hapless *Red Sox*, you will encounter a basic need. If your fiancé runs off with the best man, you will encounter a belonging need. If you were a manager in a company that is downsizing, you will feel the crush of the recognition needs when you apply for a job at Burger King. You may also feel other needs as well, as you have to consider how you're going to pay the rent and put food on the table.

And consider the need for security. On the night of September 10, 2001, we were a content and consumer-preoccupied complaisant society. We were the last superpower. Because of us the world was a reliable and orderly place. No one was going to mess with us. Well, all that smugness had evaporated by the night of September 11.

A last point about the hierarchy of needs. We have the stereotype of the "starving artist" and the creatively driven person who puts the self-actualization of art before any of the other needs. I suppose this is true in part—people endowed with creative gifts pay a price in the currency of ordinary living—but Maslow suggested that the needs lower in the hierarchy are more powerful at any one moment than the needs higher in the hierarchy.

Let's take an example. I like to think it it's a typical example. So there's this writer, but he hasn't been doing much writing lately. He's one of those people who want to be at the top of the bestseller charts without having to do any work writing. But tonight he regrets the tome he wasted. Tonight he's going to stay home and write chapter one of the Great American Novel. This is self-actualization at its finest. God and Darwin are in the bleachers applauding. But the basic needs get in the way. He suddenly becomes voraciously hungry—he'll make a sandwich first and write after dinner. The security needs get in the way. He hears someone trying to jimmy the lock on the fire escape window—he reaches for the handgun he keeps in the top right drawer of the desk. The belonging needs get in the way. A friend calls and asks why he isn't at the club. He tells his friend that he's writing chapter one of the Great American Novel. His friend tells him that Julia is at the club. He powers the laptop down. "I'll be right there," he informs his friend. And the achievement needs get in the way. The vice president at the firm he works at has given him a project. It's due in a few days. His notes for the novel are in one hand, his notes for the project are in the other hand. He switches hands, but the outcome is decided. In this dire economic climate the Great American Novel can wait for the ashram.

Self-actualization is a fragile process. It is easily interfered with. It is easily prevented. Sometimes the environment doesn't support a gifted person. No one takes him seriously. No one supports him. Like my second cousin's father, he has to work for a living. And self-actualization can be avoided. He may be a lazy person. He may not have the requisite knowledge how to succeed. He may not have the right connections or network of acquaintances. He may be frightened of failure. He may be frightened of success. And he may be frightened of his talents. Maslow called this last fear the "Jonah Complex" after the Biblical character who thought he wasn't good enough to preach to the locals and tried to give Jehovah the slip.

I can understand why people liked Maslow and why he was popular. Whatever it is, self-actualization is a noble concept, as it calls on us to step out of our ordinary limitations and strive to accomplish something great. But I think there are problems with self-actualization as a concept and with the objective of studying the best and the brightest.

Maslow assumed self-actualization involved creativity of whatever sort, but that may not be the case. There may be people who have no creative talents to self-actualize. And there are people who have what might be called "negative talents." There are cheats and murderers and cruel people among us. Satan is very good at what he does—maybe he's self-actualizing in an evil direction.

Objectifying self-actualization may motivate us to pursue something that doesn't exist beyond the individual talents people express. Spiders weave webs, birds build nests, beavers build dams. Creative people do what they do. Saying they self-actualize doesn't add much to the discussion. In this regard I'm reminded of a slogan on a tee shirt I saw on the Coney Island Boardwalk years ago. The slogan advised, "Live your life force." I thought about that and asked whether I was living my life force. I wasn't sure. I didn't think I was. I spent a lot of time trying to find my life force. I'm not sure I ever did. Maybe the pilot light of my life force was on the blink.

Maslow was an optimist who believed self-actualization was an endeavor that would lead to benevolent outcomes and he wanted to observe the best and the brightest. But intelligent people can do stupid things. And creative people can be cruel and malicious. When he came into office President Kennedy wanted to recruit "the best and the brightest" into his administration. Look what the best and the brightest in his cabinet accomplished. Just a catastrophe called the Vietnam War. Maybe he should have gone with the worst and the dumbest.

Let's move on and consider our second topic—hunger and eating as a typical motive.

We eat to take in energy to perform our life tasks, not to mention all the cellular activity that keeps us alive. We eat to take in calories. That's a dreaded word with an undeserved reputation. Calories provide our cells with the energy to divide and to heal and to eliminate waste and to engage in the myriad chemical processes that constitute life.

On the surface, that's a simple thing. We eat to stay alive. But the more we learn about hunger and eating, the more complicated the picture becomes. Hunger and eating involve physiological, psychological, and social-cultural factors.

Consider the physiological. The *liver* releases hormones that cause us to feel hungry. Those creaking and crackling noises we hear inside our bellies when we're hungry come from the liver. The liver also releases hormones that cause us to feel full. The feeling of being bloated gets us to stop eating, supposedly.

The *hypothalamus* is involved in the regulation of hunger. There's a site called the lateral hypothalamus that stimulates eating. The site is like an "on switch." We know that because when the lateral hypothalamus is destroyed in experiments, the animal will starve to death. Cats will sit and yawn when a mouse walks pass. Rats wouldn't get off the couch. There's another site called the ventro-medial hypothalamus that suppresses eating. This site is like an "off switch." If this site is destroyed the animal will eat voraciously and triple its body size in a short period of time. Imagine if we tripled our weight in a few months. We would be on the cover of *Oprah* magazine and Richard Simmons would emerge from retirement to be our weight coach. I'd like to stress that human eating disorders are not caused by a malfunctioning hypothalamus. They are caused by social factors and reflect learning more than they do physiology.

There are *homeostatic processes* at play in the regulation of eating. Some processes are psychological. We eat too much, we feel bloated. We don't eat, we're motivated to find food. We gain a few pounds, our pants feel snug and we cut back on dessert. We lose a few pounds and we have leeway to snack.

The *set point* is the body's tendency to *maintain the same weight over a period of time.* The set point is based on genetic and biological factors and it's related to metabolism, which is using up the calories we take in. We all know the blessed people who consume vast amounts of food without gaining weight. And we all know people who gain weight on a salad. The set point is based on lifestyle and on activity level and it can be slowly adjusted over time. The set point is a kind of caloric thermostat. If it falls below our correct weight, hunger increases and activity level decreases. If it rises above our correct weight, hunger decreases and activity level increases.

The set point is controversial in a physiological sense, but I think it's a useful concept in the psychological sense, as weight partially controls how we eat. And weight is adjustable based on lifestyle and activity levels. We use weight as a guide to behavior. If I may self disclose—I weigh one hundred ninety pounds. I've weighed one hundred ninety pounds for a long time. I suppose it's my set point. If I stand on the scale one morning and weigh one hundred ninety five pounds, I panic and hate myself. If I stand on the scale another morning and weigh one hundred eighty five pounds, I congratulate myself and think, "Good, you can treat yourself to a chocolate raspberry linzer bar."

There are physiological homeostatic processes at play in the regulation of eating. The most prominent is the relationship between *glucose* and *insulin*. Let's see how the two relate with a typical example. You're in class. It's late in the day and you haven't eaten for a while. You're feeling weak. Your liver is forwarding messages. Prof. Ford is on a roll. At break time you run to the cafeteria and consume a few snacks to perk up. A chocolate bar, a bag of chips, maybe a plate of stringy fries. Glucose is "blood sugar," as it's called. After you've consumed all those snacks, glucose levels are high. You're ready for the second half of the lecture.

Glucose is available energy. Glucose amounts to calories at work. But as Walter Cannon pointed out, the body is wiser than we are. It doesn't like glucose levels to be too high, so it releases insulin from the pancreas. Insulin converts excess glucose into glycogen or stored energy that can be used later, maybe on the ride home. But now the level of insulin is too high and the body doesn't like that either. Insulin makes you feel hungry. After class you run down for another snack to restore glucose.

The body likes to keep the levels of glucose and insulin balanced. If glucose is high relative to insulin, insulin is released. If insulin is high relative to glucose, we are motivated to eat and restore the level of glucose. In the ideal circumstance, everything is kept in balance.

There are psychological factors operating in the regulation of eating. Positive reinforcement plays a role. Food tastes good, food smells good, food looks good. What could be finer than a chocolate raspberry linzer bar? Or what could be finer than a bowl of spaghetti with two spicy meatballs half sunk in marinara sauce?

Think of the social aspects of food. My family sits down to supper. My co-workers go to lunch. I encounter someone I find attractive. I ask this person, "Can I take you to dinner?" If she declines the invitation, I ask, "Can you take me to dinner?" That might catch her off guard.

Negative reinforcement plays a role when it comes to eating. Negative reinforcement is defined as an increase in the rate of a response that reduces aversive stimuli. Some people have learned to hit the refrigerator and overeat when they get worried or flustered or nervous or stressed out or when their lives get out of order. We get nervous—we overeat. We get anxious—we overeat. We get harried and flustered—we overeat. We regret what we do, but we can't help ourselves. Remember the principle of immediacy. Immediate consequences are more powerful than future consequences. Food calms us down in the here and now. Carbohydrates have a tranquilizing effect by stimulating the neurotransmitter serotonin. That's more effective than what happens tomorrow morning when we step on the scale. We hate ourselves for putting on weight, but that's tomorrow. What we do today, what we do now, takes precedence. Sufficient to the day are the number of reinforcements received.

I hope you see the way negative reinforcement works. We become nervous and anxious. We eat or overeat. We grow calm and relaxed.

What reduces the nervousness and the anxiety increases in rate. Next time we feel nervous or anxious, we reach for the linzer bar. Maybe we overreach. We've learned to comfort ourselves with food.

Classical conditioning plays a role in the regulation of eating. We learn to associate certain places—like the couch—with eating. In this example the couch serves as the conditioned stimulus, food serves as the unconditioned stimulus, and eating serves as the unconditioned and conditioned responses. We sit on the couch, turn on the television, and eating comes instantly to mind.

Has it ever happened to you that you became self-aware and caught yourself eating while lying on the couch and watching the tube? It happened to me recently. I was on the couch watching some show and snacking. It suddenly dawned on me that I wasn't the least bit hungry, but I was eating anyway. And eating crazily. I like to think that, becoming self-aware, I stopped eating and put the snack away.

We associate certain visual stimuli with eating—like the big and little hands of a clock. The clock says it's five to twelve and we instantly think, "Lunch." The clock says it's five to six and we instantly think, "Supper." We may not be hungry, but the clock says what it says and we have to obey.

Social-cultural factors influence what and how we eat. Some cultures do not eat cows. Some cultures do not eat pigs. In America we eat both cows and pigs. Sometimes we eat cows and pigs at the same meal. In America we do not eat frogs or dogs. But there are cultures that eat frogs and dogs. For all I know these cultures eat frogs and dogs at the same meal.

Consider two recent phenomena in America. Twenty years ago the vegetarian lifestyle was not particularly common. Back then, being a vegetarian was looked on as a weird and unmanly custom. Today, nearly every restaurant in America offers vegetarian meals. The finest restaurants on Second Ave. offer vegetarian dishes. So do the restaurants where I dine. Burger King, for example, offers a veggie burger to go with the fries and the milk shake.

And consider the phenomenon involving the over-sizing of portions in restaurants. This phenomenon certainly plays a role in the over-sizing of Americans. The larger the portion, the more we consume. The larger the portion, the faster we eat. It is now common in restaurants to serve so much food it cannot be eaten at one sitting. The leftovers are taken home in what use to be called a "doggie bag." The current term is "box" without reference to a canine. The leftovers are consumed as a second meal. Sometimes they are consumed as a third meal. I know a restaurant that serves so much baked ziti, they take five dollars off the bill if a customer consumes everything on the plate. There is so much ziti, the bowl cannot be carried. It has to be rolled on a cart. Two servers have to lift it onto the table. Five dollars is routinely taken off the bill. I'm not going to tell you where this restaurant is located because I might see you there.

In recent years three eating disorders have become prominent in America. The media focuses on them. So does the medical profession. Two are food restrictive. These are *anorexia nervosa*, which is defined as *a severe food restriction to the point of starvation*, and *bulimia nervosa*, which is defined as *a pattern of binge eating followed by purging in the attempt to control weight*. Ninety percent of food-restrictive individuals are female. The third eating disorder is food indulgent. This, of course, is *obesity*, which is defined as being 20% over the recommended weight for gender, age, and height. As with food-restrictive eating disorders, women are more likely than men to be obese.

Anorexia nervosa is a serious psychological disorder. Often it requires hospitalization. It is a potentially fatal disorder, as the young lady does not take in sufficient nutrients to maintain her biological functions. Chief characteristics of this disorder involve significant weight loss, an intense fear of gaining weight, and a disturbance in how the body is viewed. In former centuries anorexia often occurred in a religious context, as in fasting and mortifying the flesh. Today in the industrialized world anorexia occurs in a secular context and involves dieting and disturbances in a person's self-image. These young ladies perceive themselves as overweight or in need of losing additional weight. It is a disquieting experience to talk with a person who is broomstick thin, but who insists she is fat.

Bulimia is a more common disorder and more accessible to understanding. Bulimia may not be a constant issue, but a periodical issue. Bulimia involves a pattern of binging—serious over-eating—followed by an attempt to control weight gain by some method of purging. The attempts at purging can be very variable. In former years purging involved the use of laxatives and of emetics, which are drugs that induce vomiting. In recent years purging involves the use of diet pills, which are essentially amphetamines that speed up metabolism. The use of amphetamines is dangerous and life-threatening. A famous diet pill was pulled from the market a few years ago because it triggered heart attacks. There is also a contemporary version of bulimia that involves excessive exercise as the attempt to control weight.

In former years bulimia was seen as a white woman's problem, but that is no longer the case. The pressures that create bulimia have infiltrated every race and ethnicity including women of color and Latino women.

Binging and purging are unhealthy patterns that can lead to vitamin deficiencies, weight oscillation, and dangerous, if not deadly, attempts to control weight. Like anorexic women, bulimic women experience disturbances in their body images. They see themselves as overweight. I'm sure many young men have had the experience of telling their girlfriends, "You're thin," and hearing in reply, "I'm fat." The answer to this is "You look just right."

We shouldn't minimize the importance of body image problems or body satisfaction and dissatisfaction. Some years ago the magazine *Psychology Today* conducted a survey of more than four thousand subscribers. Eighty-nine percent of female responders indicated that they wanted to lose weight. Twenty-two percent of male responders indicated they wanted to lose weight. The same survey found that obese individuals reported being teased throughout their lives about being overweight. The survey also found that media models were influential. The responders wanted to look like the beautiful people they see in movies and in magazines. We should keep in mind that responders may have presented a biased sample and one that is thinner than members of the lumpen class who don't subscribe to *Psychology Today*.

The pressures that lead to bulimia affect all age groups—bulimia is no longer a young woman's problem. There are cases of bulimic children—of girls not yet pubescent and as young as nine and ten years. At the opposite end of the age spectrum a survey of women in their sixties that ranked fears found the following. This group of older women ranked Alzheimer's as the number one fear. Cancer was ranked third. Gaining weight was ranked second. This is amazing. Being overweight—believing that you are overweight—is more frightening than cancer.

I want to stress that the factors that contribute to dissatisfaction with one's body and to bulimia are not biological but thoroughly social-cultural. Our culture places great value on thinness—it equates beauty with being thin. This development began after World War Two, so it's a relatively recent change. In the 1960s there was a sexpot in the movies named Marilyn Monroe. Maybe you heard of her. There are stills from her last and unfinished movie that show her in a bikini. Her belly is folded over the top of her bikini bottom. The voluptuous Marilyn Monroe had the makings of a pot belly. This would never be tolerated in any glamorous star in Tinsel Town today. The sexpots of today are lucky they have any flesh on their bellies, still less a budding roll of flab.

Our culture not only equates beauty with thinness, it actively stigmatizes obesity. Think of the stereotypes of the heavy person in movies—they're either thugs or clowns. "Fatty" is made fun of growing up, "Skinny" is not. This view of obesity as gross or obscene extends, sadly enough, to the pharmaceutical industry. A televised ad for Lipozene, a diet pill, claims—this is a quote, I put the snacks down and wrote it when I heard it—"Body fat is unattractive."

Our culture interprets losing weight as an accomplishment and gaining weight as a moral failure. If you tell me, "I lost ten pounds," I say, "Great, how'd you do it?" If you tell me, "I gained ten pounds," I say, "I'm sorry to hear that" and I think, "Wow, you sure let yourself go." Losing weight is seen as an expression of character—a person has self-discipline. Gaining weight is seen as a character defect—a person doesn't have self-discipline.

Our culture presents highly influential and highly unrealistic images of beauty. Women in real life do not look like the models on the cover of *Cosmopolitan*. They can't look like those models. And men in real life do not look like the models on the cover of *GQ*. They can't look like those models. We forget that the models on the covers of magazines live unusual lifestyles. Some images have been created by plastic surgery. Some images have been touched up by editors. The average female model is 20% thinner than 95% of American females. Only one-in-one hundred thousand 5'7 women have the 39-23-33 dimensions of the Barbie doll. This woman lives in New Jersey. Fewer men have the torso of GI Joe.

Bulimia runs in families. We now have families in which three generations show bulimic eating patterns. Grandmother, mother, and daughter are bulimic. It's not necessarily the case that bulimia is taught by the parents. It may be a case of unconscious modeling and conformity, like when an offspring takes up smoking or drinking because the parents smoke or drink. It may be the case that one sister learns the bulimic pattern from another sister. In this case the transmission may be more explicit. One sister says to the other, "I'm gaining weight." The implication is that "I'm not attractive." The other sister may advise her what to do—go to a doctor and order Lipozene.

Interestingly, the same process may occur in alcoholic families. Yes, there is a positive correlation between fathers and sons drinking. There is an even stronger positive correlation between siblings drinking. If an older brother drinks, the chances increase that the younger brother drinks. It's less likely that the father gives his son the keys to the liquor cabinet. It's more likely that the older brother tells the younger brother how to get alcohol.

When it comes to bulimia the same explicit learning or modeling occurs among friends and peer groups who tell one another what to do in the God-awful situation when one of them gains weight. Many young women do not acquire bulimic eating patterns until they leave home and live in dormitories at college or in a barracks in the military. A friend may know about diet pills and, when asked, is only too happy to share this knowledge. That's what friends are for.

I think you can see the pressure many young women face—what women of every age face. They believe they must be thin to be attractive. They think weight gain is a personal failing. The media bombards them with unrealistic images. These pressures happen in a place rich with food. Restrictive eating disorders occur in food-rich cultures. They tend not to happen in places where food is scarce. The country of New York has a restaurant on nearly every block. If not a restaurant, then a fast-food joint. If not a fast-food joint, then a bodega. And in the midst of this plenty, the young woman is supposed not to indulge.

Finally, these pressures are exacerbated by puberty. When girls go through puberty, they put on weight. Their hips widen, their breasts emerge. To start with, girls have more adipose (fat) tissue than boys. Now it's a great thing to become mature. They're no longer a "girl," but a "young woman." Boys find them attractive. They can go on dates. Becoming mature can also be a troubling event. They are told directly and indirectly that it's not a good thing to put on weight.

In all eating disorders, whether anorexia, bulimia, or obesity, there is *a disconnect between eating and feeling hungry*. The average four year old can do what the average adult can't—eat only when hungry. If the four year old doesn't feel hungry, he or she is not the least bit interested in eating. No amount of pleading or prodding can pull the average four year old from his or her toys. When the four year old is hungry, the world comes to a stop. "Mommy, I'm hungry." "Mommy, I'm hungry." They don't want to do anything else but eat. When they're hungry, they're not the least bit interested in toys.

Compare their behavior to that of the average adult. Adults often eat when they're not hungry. Adults often overeat when they're not the least bit hungry. And adults often fend off the pangs of hunger, as in anorexia and, more commonly, when they go on diets. With all their strength, dieters try to resist temptation. They're stronger than that chocolate raspberry linzer bar that's bewitching them. Or so they like to think.

In anorexia and in bulimia we find food restrictions—we don't eat when we are hungry. *Obesity* shares the same dynamic—hunger and eating have become disconnected—but it involves taking in more food than we require. It may also involve an element of inactivity.

Obesity is defined as being 20% over the recommended weight range for gender, age, and height. Obesity is defined as an index of thirty points and greater in terms of the Body Mass Index that we can find on line. There are, of course, controversies involving these weight ranges that are established by medical organizations, insurance companies, and diet services, such as Weight Watchers. These ranges may understate acceptable weights for tall people, for example, and they do not address issues of health and activity.

However defined, there is no question that obesity has increased over the past quarter century. Some estimates place this increase at 25%. Since 1960 the average American is one inch taller and twenty three pounds heavier. Estimates suggest that a whopping 30% of the American population is obese. A few years back, it was estimated that 30% of the Navy was overweight. I'm not making this figure up—I saw the figure in an article written by the *chief* chief petty officer. (In recent years the Army has complained that many recruits are so out of shape they cannot pass the physical requirements to enter the service.) One-in-three American children is overweight—that's 33%. Twenty years ago the New York City Transit System replaced the seventeen inch fanny sized seat with flat open seats. Presumably, more riders can squeeze their fannies in on the ride to and from school.

The situation isn't unique to America. Unlike restrictive food disorders that are not common in poor countries, some of the world's highest rates of obesity are in the poorest countries. This is because of the high intake of soda and of foods rich in sugar. It's estimated that, world wide, half a billion people are obese.

The contributing factors to this explosion of obesity in America aren't difficult to identify. We eat high-sugar, high-fat foods, we drink too much soda, and we have become inactive. In America we eat oversized portions. The larger the portion, the more we eat. As I mentioned, I frequent a restaurant where the servers have to be weightlifters to haul the dishes to the dinner table. Recently, I stopped at a fast-food restaurant on Chambers St. The clerk asked if I wanted a soda with my six-inch roast beef sandwich on herbs and spices bread. I said I wanted the small size soda. The clerk handed me a cup that was more than a foot tall. This was the *small* size. If I ordered the large size, I'd have to start lifting weights.

Generally, people underestimate the calories they take in. Starting in 2008 New York City required restaurants and bakeries to post the calories of the portions they serve. Mayor Bloomberg was roundly criticized for this, but posting calories is an effective way to get people to consider what they consume. Surveys indicate that about 25% of customers use the postings to guide their choices.

In America we mostly work at sedentary occupations. Many people sit in front of a keyboard all day and exercise only the muscles in their fingers. We don't do physical labor, not in the way our ancestors did. If we want to do anything physical, we have to set aside a chunk of time and go to a place called a "health spa." The longshoreman I mentioned in the context of self-actualization didn't need to go to a spa to get physical. His occupation involved working out.

There may be hereditary factors that predispose people to gaining weight. And eating habits early in childhood may cause fat cells to multiply. Fat cells do not vanish when the person goes on a diet—they shrink. Presumably, they want to get back to full size.

The disconnect between hunger and eating may commence in the preschool years. I can see situations where mothers, in trying to be helpful, force their children to eat when they're not hungry. "Ma, I'm not hungry," the child says. "Yes, you are. Now eat," Ma replies, forcing food on the child. I can also see the reverse situation. The child is gripped in the agony of hunger. "Ma, I'm hungry." "Wait till supper," Ma insists.

I can also see the situation in which children learn to comfort and calm themselves with food. This habit can carry on through life. As with adults, many children have become sedentary. If there was such a place, they'd have to go to a juvenile health spa to do anything physical.

There is another factor that contributes to obesity and this involves the brain. Leptin is a hormone secreted from fat cells that suppresses eating by making us feel full. Leptin tells the hypothalamus that we have sufficient energy (calories) and that it's time to stop eating. This process may be overridden by the consumption of foods rich in sugar and fat. Such high-caloric foods involve a pleasure center of the brain, specifically the striatum, an organ located deep in the brain. Such foods stimulate the striatum to increase the neurotransmitters dopamine and endorphins. These neurotransmitters, in turn, inspire continued consumption of food.

The process that leads to obesity may involve a depressed striatum— obese individuals may have to eat more food to derive pleasure from eating. Or the process may involve reduced dopamine receptors, causing the necessity of higher levels of dopamine to gain a positive effect. Whatever the process, this disruption of the ordinary feedback in eating resembles addiction to cocaine and to alcohol. (The striatum is involved in these addictions.) The more an obese person eats, the more he or she craves, since the shut-down or slow-down process is disrupted.

Recent research has suggested that the bacteria in our digestive systems may play a contributing role in obesity. The bacteria in lean people are more diverse than the bacteria in obese people—this may have to do with the consumption of sugar and processed food. One bacterium—*Heliobacter pylori*—played a role in controlling weight by regulating a hormone called ghrelin, which stimulates hunger. Unfortunately, *H. pylori* is now uncommon in our guts. Ghrelin is less well regulated and we feel hungry more frequently. Incidentally, the disappearance of *H. pylori* is attributed to the overuse of antibiotics.

Whatever the origin of obesity—surely, it is caused by an interaction of a number of factors—obesity poses substantial health risks. Published reports that obesity contributed to hundreds of thousands of deaths have been questioned, but obesity is a potent risk factor in heart disease, high blood pressure, and diabetes. Obesity is linked to an inactive lifestyle. Obese individuals may not have the ability or the stamina to get around with ease. They may not be able to participate in sports or in the kinds of activities that would help keep their weight under better control.

There's good news and there's bad news when it comes to dieting. The bad news is that dieters seldom keep the weight off. Not after the first diet. Not after the second diet. Maybe not after the third diet. The good news is that losing weight is like becoming sober from addiction to drugs and alcohol. Relapsing is considered part of the recovery process. Relapsing is considered part of the dieting process. We may fall off the wagon and land at the dinner table, but diets can succeed if we persist.

The keys to losing weight and to keeping weight off are to reduce food intake slightly and to increase activity level slightly. The motto is "*Eat less, move more.*" I'll like to stress the word "slightly." Small changes can result in appreciable gains—I should say appreciable losses.

Here are a few things we can do to reduce food intake. Reduce the amount of bread that we eat. Some people eat six slices a day and that's nearly half a loaf. Reduce the calories that come from sweets and from fats. Reduce the number of snacks. If we must snack, eat trail mix and raisins rather than beer pretzels and chips. Reduce the amount of soda we consume. Some people consume three or four cans a day. In the 1950s the standard size soda container in fast-food restaurants was seven ounces. Today, the standard size soda container is sixteen ounces. Reduce the size of the portions we consume. The larger the portion, the more we eat. The larger the portion, the faster we eat. Use smaller plates, use smaller glasses. Plate size may make a difference in how much we eat. The larger the plate, the more food we place on it. Reducing plate size by two inches decreases serving size by 20%. Reduce plate size and use red plates. Strange as this sounds, people eat less food off red plates than off any other color plate. Try not to eat when stressed or in a hurry. I know we have hectic lives, but try not to "eat on the run." Try to become aware of the state of your body. When we sit to eat, we can ask ourselves if we really feel hungry.

Don't avoid meals. Some people attempt to diet by eating only one meal, but this strategy can be counterproductive, since it runs the risk of overeating at that meal and of reducing metabolism. Remember that metabolism is adjustable. The less we eat, the slower metabolism becomes. A better strategy is to eat lightly throughout the day in order to maintain a normal metabolism. The operative word, of course, is "lightly."

In terms of activity level, we don't need to join a health spa. We just need to move more. Get outside. Walk more. If it's a safe neighborhood and if we're not being stalked by thuggish types, we can get off one subway station before our stop and walk the rest of the way. Walk up one flight rather than taking the escalator. Do you know there are students in this building who take the elevator rather than walk up one flight?

The reason why we want to increase activity level is to keep our metabolism at an active level. When we maintain an active lifestyle while dieting, we maintain an active metabolism. We burn up calories and lose weight. When we go on a diet and do not increase activity level—when we stay at the same lethargic level as before—our metabolism slowly decreases. This decrease is fine so long as there is reduced food intake. When we reach our desired weight and return to normal eating or when we drift from the diet and—ehem—let ourselves go, we put on weight rapidly because our metabolism has slowed. We become disappointed because all our hard work has gone for nothing.

The key to successful dieting is to reduce food intake and to stay active or to become active. The latter ensures that the metabolism stays high and the set point does not lower. If we eat less and move more, we'll lose weight and keep it off. If we do that, we'll look good and feel good as we visit the salad bar in the food court at the local mall.

Thank you.

Tips to Students ~
Taking Lecture Notes

Go to all classes and stay the entire class. Many instructors make important announcements at the end of class. Try to sit near the front center of the room.

Take notes on everything the instructor emphasizes. Write *everything* the instructor puts on the board or displays in a power point presentation. Record the instructor's examples *exactly* as they are given.

Train yourself to concentrate on what is being said. Be alert for possible quiz items, such as the instructor saying, "This may be on the quiz," or "You may see this again." Most instructors make it a point to cover everything that will be on the quiz.

If you are absent, try to copy someone else's notes. But remember that they will not be as good as your own notes.

Write clearly and date your notes. Try to develop abbreviations of common words and frequently recurring terms. Take notes on one side of the page. Keep your ideas separate from the class notes so the two are not confused. It might be useful to place your ideas in brackets.

As soon as possible after class, take time to review the notes. If something is unclear, or if it appears you missed something, place a question mark next to the item and ask the instructor. While reviewing the class notes you can revisit the ideas placed in brackets and decide whether they may be something you'd want to elaborate. It may be that you can address some of these ideas with the instructor.

LECTURE THREE ~

Emotions

I'll like to introduce the study of emotions by a review of the topic in the history of psychology. If we look at the psychology textbooks of the late nineteenth and early twentieth centuries, we'll find emotion a prominent topic and one that merited entire chapters. Take, for example, *Principles of Psychology* by William James. If we then review the textbooks of the middle twentieth century, we'll find that emotion is mostly gone from the books. The only exception is anxiety, which makes sense considering the events of the middle of the twentieth century.

What happened in American psychology to banish emotion was the rise of behaviorism. Behaviorists disliked dealing with subjective variables like feelings or moods. I believe behaviorism to be one of the oddest developments in American psychology, but behaviorists made cogent criticisms of the study of emotion. They claimed, and rightly, that emotions can be *posed* and *faked*, which are no minor obstacles to their study. Emotions can also be *masked*, in which one emotion conceals a second emotion. For example, anger sometimes conceals fear and happiness sometimes conceals sadness.

Faking emotions doesn't only happen in the sack, when she screams "Yes!" at the top of her voice and pretends he's tops among lover boys. Faking emotions happen all the time. Consider what happened to me recently. We went to the funeral parlor. A distant relative twice removed on the paternal side had passed away. I never met this person in life. In fact, the only time I saw him was in the casket. I knew what I was supposed to do. I put a suit on and my best grief face. I bowed my head, grimaced, and spoke in a choke of a whisper. I played the part of a grieving relative so convincingly his widow comforted me.

And consider what happened when I visited Macy's back in the day I was buying chocolate raspberry linzer bars by the bag full. I had to cross the cologne stalls on the main floor to get to the bakery. A line of beautiful young women were smiling at me and holding bottles of cologne. They were trying to spray me with samples of the scents. How could I turn them down? I thought they were smiling exclusively at me. I thought they liked me. Later, I learned that they smiled at all the male customers—I think I must have looked back one time and saw one of the ladies smiling at a different customer. I was very disappointed. Their smiles were obviously fixed and fake. Like everyone in retail, they hated customers and wished we would go away and die. But they had to fake a smile to make a sale and earn their commission.

Regardless that the smiles were posed, they were effective in getting me to buy cologne. I have enough bottles of cologne in the bathroom closet to last for the rest of my life.

The idea that emotions—emotional displays—are effective despite the fact that we know the emotions are posed and faked is called *emotion work*. These posed emotions are part of social intercourse. The widow expects mourners to wear the grief face. Customers expect salesladies to wear smiles. Similarly, diners in restaurants expect the servers to smile. People in airplanes expect the flight attendants to smile—all right, people in airplanes don't expect that. In the social psychology lecture I'll introduce a concept called the *fundamental attribution error*. We tend to attribute emotional expressions to the personalities of the people who wear them— to mourners and to salesladies—rather than to the situations—wakes, department stores—the people are participating in.

Behaviorists advanced additional criticisms of the study of emotion. How many emotions are there? Are there basic emotions that are not divisible into simpler emotions? Are there blends of emotions that could be mixed like the ingredients in a stew? Are some emotions fixed in biology? Are other emotions social constructs? What is the temporal duration of emotions? Some emotions last for a few seconds, like the happiness following a joke. Other emotions last for a great while, like the sadness that accompanies major depression. Some emotions are voluntary and under conscious control—we say "we have" these emotions. Other emotions are involuntary and outside conscious control—we say "they have" us. Are some emotions beyond conscious experience? Psychodynamic psychologists made a good living kayaking the unconscious sea in search of those. Can language handle emotions adequately? There are, for example, different kinds of anger and disgust, yet we use the same words to denote different emotions.

There's a final nuance that may have turned behaviorists off the study of emotion. The expression of emotion, of strong emotion particularly, has often been judged as dangerous and primitive. We don't feel comfortable seeing an angry person or a person stricken with grief. We don't know what to do in these situations. We don't know how to react. Emotions are hot. They're threatening. In the grip of strong emotions—of emotions that "have us"—we are in danger of losing control. We tell an emotionally aroused person to "calm down" and to "get a grip." We tell the same things to ourselves when we feel we are in danger of "losing it." Who knows what bad things can happen when we lose it? We don't stick around long enough to find out.

Let's return to the historical overview. Emotions came back into psychology in a major way in the 1970s by piggybacking on the study of nonverbal communication, which was one of the hottest research topics of the time. Researchers used videotape machines to record and analyze the nonverbal communications that occur in interpersonal situations. Researchers could film people as they interacted face-to-face. The film could be run in slow motion. The film could be stopped. It could be run over and over. Emotions are obviously an important element of interpersonal behavior. I wonder how behaviorists could have missed so elemental a fact.

Modern psychology suggests that there a limited number of *basic emotions*. Depending on the theory a person favors, this number varies between six and twelve. The basic emotions can be combined to form the myriad emotions we experience as we go through the day.

The basic emotions are part of our biological endowment. Charles Darwin and others believed they are part of our evolutionary history. Darwin believed we share these emotions with other primates. In 1872 he published an interesting book called *The Expression of the Emotions in Man and Animals*. The basic emotions are believed to be universal among people. Cultures vary in what they name emotions and in how freely people are allowed to express emotions, but the basic emotions occur in all people. The people in the northern-most quadrant of the Bronx express the same basic emotions as the people who live in Coney Island. If I were transported backward in time to the court of Cleopatra, I would recognize the surprise on her face as I beamed in. And she would recognize the fear on my face.

In the 1960s an isolated tribe was identified living in New Guinea that had never seen American (non-tribal) faces in the memory of anyone in the tribe. They had never seen photographs of American faces. They had never seen television. The tribe was called the Fore people. Members of the tribe were able to identify the emotions in photographs of American faces. Presumably, they were able to identify the emotions on the faces of the researchers. They accurately named every emotion—in their own language, of course. I'm not sure I'm happy to report that the Fore tribe is now like everyone else on Earth. They have television now and can watch reruns of *Hogan's Heroes* and *My Mother, the Car*.

Regardless of the number of basic emotions, every emotion has the same components—*physiological arousal, conscious experience,* and *verbal* and *nonverbal expression*.

Physiological arousal includes as a primary component autonomic nervous system activity.

Conscious experience includes moods and the subjective experience of emotion—this is what the behaviorists objected to. It also includes attributions—what we tell ourselves about what we are feeling and why we are feeling that way.

Expression is what we show of our emotions. We tell others how we feel. "I feel sad today." "Yesterday, I was happy." "I was disgusted the day before that." Our faces are fixed in certain ways as we describe our emotions. The volume and pitch of our voices change. So do the gestures we make.

Expression sets up the context in which our words are appraised. If I say, "I feel sad," and make a frown, you believe I do, in fact, feel sad. If I say, "I feel sad," while smiling cheerily, you probably do not believe that I feel sad. If I say, "I feel happy," while smiling cheerily, you believe me. If I say, "I'm happy," while tears are streaming down my cheeks, you probably do not believe me, unless I were the featured guest in a bridal shower. But I don't think you'd believe me in that particular role.

I'll like to describe two topics that fall under the heading of arousal. By arousal I mean general physiological arousal rather than sexual arousal. The topics are the relation of arousal to optimum task performance and to lie detection. Then I'll like to move onto the emotions of anger and happiness and describe a few general principles that apply to emotions. I'll describe the James-Lange theory of emotion in its original format and in its revised format. I'll conclude the topic of emotion by describing the importance of the face in regulating emotions.

The relationship between arousal and performance depends on the nature of the task. It is better to be in a state of *lower arousal* when we perform *complex tasks or tasks that are newly learned*. It is better to be in a state of *higher arousal* when we perform *simple tasks or tasks that are well learned*.

When performing complex tasks we need to stay in the proverbial "calm, cool, collected" state. I don't want my surgeon to be in a state of agitation when he resections my small intestines. When performing simple tasks we need some of the proverbial "get up and go" to perform successfully. I don't want my barber to be overly lethargic while he styles my hair.

The relationship of arousal and task complexity has obvious implication for study habits. When you read a new chapter or study a new topic, it is important to be in a state of lower arousal. Shut the television off. Shut the cell phones off. Send the kids to the movies. Send the spouse to the living room. It's not easy—it may not even be possible—to study effectively in a busy and noisy environment. On the other hand, you may need some noise and something in the way of a warm up when you are reviewing a topic you're familiar with.

If I may be permitted to self disclose—no, I'm not going to self disclose what happened in Las Vegas last November. It's something much less exciting. I've been teaching general psychology for many years. I vividly recall my first general psychology class. It was in this very building—every class since has been in this building. I had never taught a class before. I wasn't sure what I was doing. I didn't want to make a mistake and shame myself in front of students. I wrote the lecture longhand. I rehearsed it so I would finish on time. I practiced it in front of my family. I practiced using a videocassette recorder.

My problem now is the reverse. I've taught general psychology so many times I know the lectures nearly word-for-word. I need to motivate myself so I perform at an optimum level. To accomplish this, I warm up in the department office. I do forty one-arm pushups with my right hand. I do forty one-arm pushups with my left hand. I do forty jumping jacks. I do forty squat thrusts. I race around the building at maximum speed. And then I'm ready to lecture. The glass of whiskey helps, too.

There is a wrinkle on arousal and task performance that derives from social psychology. This is the concept of *social facilitation*. It works like this. When we are confident and sure of what we're doing, we like to perform with other people and in front of other people. The presence of other people facilitates the performance of well-learned tasks. When we are not confident and not sure of ourselves, we prefer to work alone and without the presence of spectators. The presence of other people inhibits and complicates performance.

We like an audience when we're sure of ourselves and of our abilities. Other people inspire us and rouse us to new levels. We prefer isolation when we're not sure of ourselves and our abilities. I suppose it's a self-respect thing. We don't like people to see us fail. It's okay to fail, but only in private.

The next topic I'll like to introduce under the heading of arousal is *lie detection*. The lie detector machine—the *polygraph*—monitors physiological arousal—blood pressure, heart rate, breathing, skin conductance. The person taking the test is asked a series of questions. Changes in the state of arousal of the person's autonomic nervous system are conjectured to mark the points at which the person is lying.

The polygraph machine was introduced in America in the 1920s. Throughout the 1980s more than a million tests were administered in the United States. Currently, the use of the test has been curtailed in many professions and courtrooms. Despite problems with the test and several spectacular failures to identify traitors in their midst, the FBI, CIA, and the Defense Department continue to administer the polygraph thousands of times yearly. They do this in the hiring practice and in random screening of employees.

The logic of the polygraph machine is tight. A liar is able to control his or her voice. "Did you take money from the cash register?" the examiner asks. The liar's voice remains steady. "I most certainly did not." A liar is able to control his or her facial expression. "Did you take money from the cash register?" The facial expression of indignation doesn't change. A liar is able to control his or her gestures. "Did you take money from the cash register?" The finger tapping doesn't change. "Did you take money from the cash register?" The logic of the machine suggests that the liar is not able to control autonomic nervous system processes for the good reason that he or she does not know what is going on physiologically.

We don't know what our blood pressure is or what our heart rate is or what our breathing capacity is or what our skin conductance is. Right now, our hearts are doing something. Right now, our livers are up to something. Right now, our small intestines are hard at work. We don't know what any of the visceral organs are doing until they stop doing it, at which time we are in big trouble.

The logic appears tight, but it is anything but tight. The logic is rather loose. There is little empirical evidence to support the claim that the polygraph identifies lies with high reliability. As far back as 1998 the Supreme Court concluded, "There is simply no consensus that polygraph evidence is reliable." The National Academy of Science concluded in 2003 that "Almost a century of research in scientific psychology and physiology provides little basis for the expectation that a polygraph test could have extremely high accuracy."

Polygraphs do not identify lies. *Polygraphs identify arousal.* Arousal is not the same as deceit. Arousal may accompany deceit. Arousal may be present when there is no deceit. And arousal may be absent when deceit occurs.

Polygraphs err about one-fourth of the time. This is an unacceptably high error rate—it's a spectacular error rate. In the 1980s this was a quarter million errors yearly. Imagine if a medical test erred 25% of the time. It would be withdrawn from practice immediately. In some cases errors are *false positives* or *false alarms*—truthful individuals are judged as lying. In other cases errors are *false negatives* or *misses*—liars are judged as telling the truth. The accuracy of the tests increases when the questions are specific and involve specific events. Asking "Did you take fifty dollars from the cash register on Monday night, July 18?" results in greater accuracy than asking, "Did you ever take money from the cash register?"

I can understand how a false positive can occur. An honest, law-abiding person is asked blunt and disturbing questions. "Did you take money from the cash register?" There is a lot riding on the answer. The person may be fired. The person may be arrested. The person becomes so stressed—stress involves arousal—that he or she *acts as if telling a lie.* The questions may be so intimidating the person answers as if telling a lie.

And I can understand how a false negative can occur. One evening years ago I went uptown to buy a chocolate raspberry linzer bar in Macy's bakery. I use to do that on a lot of evenings in those years. As I entered the store police led a group of people out the door and into a paddy wagon. All the people were chained to one another, but they weren't going to the cotton fields or to the shoulders of the interstates. They were going to central booking for the slap on the wrist to be delivered by the judge in night court. They were shoplifters who had been nabbed and held in the lockup somewhere in Macy's. If they were administered polygraphs for some reason, they wouldn't be upset at being asked, "Did you shoplift?" Every variety of criminal has a specialty and shoplifting is theirs. Shoplifting is what they do for a living. They may not be good at it, since they were nabbed, but it's their occupation. Asking questions about their occupation would hardly be upsetting or stressful.

Since polygraphs are no longer legal in many situations, corporations have resorted to the use of *Honesty Tests* in which trained interviewers pay close attention to changes in facial expression and vocalization as possible signals of deceit. A series of neutral questions is used to establish a baseline—a person's routine way of looking, acting, and speaking. Crucial test questions are then inserted in the list. "Did you get along with your co-workers?" "Did you get along with management?" "Did you come into work on time?" "Did you ever steal from your last place of employment?" The interviewer watches and notes if the person looks, acts, and speaks differently to the test questions than to the neutral questions. Does he look away when asked about stealing? Does he frown? Does he hesitate? Does the volume of his voice change? Does the pitch of his voice change? Such nonverbal changes may indicate deceit.

Or they may not. Honesty Tests have higher error rates than polygraph machines, which is why they are so frequently used.

The general public—many law enforcement agencies, too—have a misguided notion of lie detection. Probably, they derived this notion from watching too many television programs. How many times have we heard a character insist on taking a polygraph test? "Let me take a lie detector test and I'll prove I'm innocent!" But taking a lie detection test doesn't prove anything. Not with an error rate of 25%.

The fact is identifying liars is extraordinarily difficult. Paul Ekman, a prominent psychologist, has written two books on lying and he concludes that it's difficult to catch a liar in the act, especially if we don't know the person. Ekman filmed real criminals describing their crimes and non-criminals describing made-up crimes. He splices the tape, intermingling the statements of truthful criminals and deceitful non-criminals, and shows it to professionals, such as police, FBI, lawyers, judges, and psychiatrists. Can they identify the liars on the tape? In fact, they cannot. They score the same as humble college students—a fifty-fifty accuracy rate. That's scoring at the level of chance. Secret Service agents score the highest, just a bit above chance. Keep in mind that this is no parlor game or trivial finding. The criminal justice system has as one of its core tasks the identification of liars, who we want to lock away in the gray-bar hotel, and the identification of truthful people, who we want to keep on the streets.

Ordinary citizens face the same problem as people in the criminal justice system. We ask the clerk if the chocolate raspberry linzer bar on the tray is fresh and we get an answer. We suspect we're being told the truth, but we don't know for sure until we bite the chocolate. The incoming governor says taxes are coming down. We hope they are, since we're going broke paying them, but we don't know if it's campaign malarkey until we get the next tax bill in the mail. The professor says the quiz is easy. Students hope it is, since they didn't study, but they don't know if he's telling the truth until they see question number one. The guy the young lady met at the club told her he's a brain surgeon at Bellevue Hospital. She hopes he is, since she gave him her number, but she doesn't know for sure.

As you can note from these examples, we have a lot riding on sorting the truth tellers from the deceivers. We're just not very good at doing that.

Let's move onto *anger* as a prototypical emotion. If I do my job right, you'll become kindly and peace-loving people.

I chose anger as an emotion to review because everyone in your country of New York is angry. If not angry, then impatient and irritable.

You probably know the observation about tourists and Native New Yorkers. I heard this on the comedy network on cable—the station should be called the "angry network," since that's what humor has become. The jokes are nothing more than insults and rude remarks. All stand-up comics talk about—I should say complain about—is something that annoyed them on the way to the club. That's what monologues have become—a monotonous litany of complaints.

Anyway, back to the observation. It's easy to tell the difference between tourists and Native New Yorkers. Tourists wear bright clothes, they look up, and they look happy. Native New Yorkers wear dark clothes, they look down, and they look angry. I suppose with so many tourists clogging the sidewalks they have reasons to be angry.

And back to anger. *We experience anger whenever we face an obstacle or experience a drop in self-esteem.* When we feel anger, we make the angry face. Our brows are drawn together and compressed. Our mouths are rigid and clenched. Our gazes are fixed at the source of anger. The expression is called a "glare." The actor Clint Eastwood made a career of glaring.

When we experience anger, the rate of speech increases and the pitch of our voices rise. We may gesture more—maybe the term is "gesticulate." Our hands may thrust forward, as if removing the source of anger.

There are changes in the autonomic nervous system. Heart rate increases. Hormones and steroids are released into the bloodstream— we'll describe this process in the lecture on health. The temperature of our limbs increases. We get a flushed look. We are in the zone of the fight-and-flight response. That's not a particularly good place to be.

When we feel anger we are motivated to overcome or to get around the obstacle. And we are motivated to recover our self-esteem. As the interpersonal psychiatrist Harry Stack Sullivan (1892-1949) pointed out, we often recover our self-esteem by lowering it in another person. Anger turns us against people. Anger causes us to treat people as enemies.

If we consider the sources of anger, we can see why anger is so prevalent. We live hectic lives. We are constantly on the go. We are constantly encountering obstacles. The trains are late and crowded. Macy's bakery is sold out of chocolate raspberry linzer bars. There's a "traffic jam in Harlem backed up to Jackson Heights," as they sang in the old TV show. We have to be somewhere and we can't get there. We have a term paper to turn in, but the printer broke. We have a deadline to meet and we're behind schedule.

When it comes to self-esteem, we have elevated images of ourselves. We want to be considered with deference and courtesy. Think how you feel if someone steps ahead of you on the escalator. Think what happens if someone steps on your foot or brushes against you. Think how you feel if the bartender serves someone ahead of you or if the saleslady in Macy's waits on someone else. All day long on the sales floor irate customers are screaming, "I was here first!" This is followed by, "I've been shopping here for fifty years and I'm taking my business elsewhere." The sales help can't say it, but they're thinking, "Good riddance to you."

Think how we feel when we are insulted or belittled. Has it ever happened to you that you realize only later—maybe on the train ride home—that you were insulted and didn't realize it at the time? Right away, you think of all the things you would have said to recover your glorified self-image.

Anger may be so prevalent because it is part of our biological inheritance—we started out as hunters, after all. Anger may also be prevalent because it is effective as an emotion. The expression of anger is frequently reinforced. Whatever gets reinforced increases in rate. Angry people become angrier.

People generally back down to an angry person—we're choleery to confront an angry person. An angry person gets his or her way. If someone is driving aggressively, we change lanes and slow down. If someone acts up in a store, the sales help rush to wait on the person just to be rid of him or her. If someone jumps ahead of us on line outside the movie theater, we don't cause a scene. It's sensible to pick our fights rationally. Do we really want to get into a brawl over a seat in a theater?

Anger is so prevalent, a new psychiatric disorder was described in 2006. This is Intermittent Explosive Disorder. It is believed to be caused by the absence of the neurotransmitter serotonin in the amygdala of the limbic system of the brain. It involves the expression of rage and the loss of inhibition against outright aggression. Individuals experiencing Intermittent Explosive Disorder lose self-control when encountering an obstacle or suffering a blow to self-esteem. If they think we cut in front of them on line outside a movie theater, they will hunt us down and scream at us. If they think we disrespected them on the county road by driving too slow, they will risk a crash to get back at us. Maybe they cut in front of us and slam on the brakes. Maybe they try to sideswipe us. They're so full of rage they don't realize what can happen when fenders kiss at seventy five miles an hour.

That's the thing about anger. It is a dangerous emotion. For good reason the Roman Catholic Church lists wrath among the seven deadly sins. Anger can get us killed, if we're not careful. It's estimated that there are more than four hundred road rage deaths a year and more than twenty-five thousand injuries in drivers who lose control of themselves and their vehicles. Some individuals meet St. Peter and earn their halo and harp because they reacted badly to someone driving slowly. More likely, it's a meeting with Satan and the earning of a pitchfork and a spray jar of sulfur cologne.

Anger can get people killed on the sidewalks as well as on the highways. The most dangerous places in your country after dark are the sidewalks outside taverns. You know how it is. Someone gets served ahead of you. Someone takes your seat. Someone hits on your girl. Before you know it, you're exchanging words and hot glances. "Let's step outside," you say, reaching for your switchblade. You think you're tough, but you just picked a fight with a guy reaching for a handgun. But think on the bright side—your girl dresses her best for your wake.

Anger can get us killed on the highways. Anger can get us killed on the sidewalks. Anger can get us killed going through the routine process of living. *Anger affects the cardio-vascular system.* Angry people have elevated levels of stress hormones (cortisol and epinephrine). Anger elevates heart rate and blood pressure. In a study that came out of Dallas recently, anger—specifically rage—produced heart flutters that can lead to strokes. (This was true for males, but not for females.) The stereotype of a person so angry he blew a blood vessel appears to be true. Chronic anger is so damaging to the body it ranks with smoking and obesity as a risk factor in premature death.

All of us get angry. Many of us get angry frequently. Since the early 1970s researchers have identified a personality pattern in people prone to anger. This is the infamous *Type A personality.*

Type A personalities are hard-driving, impatient, competitive, and hostile people. They're the kind of person who gets irritated by small things. They work fast. They multi-task. They're driven by deadlines.

They don't like to wait on lines outside movie theaters. They don't like to get behind cars doing the speed limit. They suffer from "hurry sickness."

Think of the stereotypical Wall St. account executives. They want to close the sale and make the deal. They don't have a lot of time to negotiate. They not only want to make the deal, they want to beat out competitor firms and put them out of business. Think of the lifestyle of these account executives. They're always under pressure. They eat on the run. Probably, they eat junk food. They smoke and drink and socialize with other cut-throat executives. They are sleep deprived. They have to schedule time to exercise. They have to schedule time to be pleasant.

Hostility may be the crucial characteristic that demarcates Type A personalities from ordinary angry people—the rest of us. Type A personalities are not only angry, they're angry and hostile. Maybe they should have been called Type H personalities.

Type A personalities earn their pitchforks and spray jars of sulfur cologne ahead of the rest of us. Studies show that these hostile people die prematurely. I should say they have increased risk of dying prematurely given their age and cohort. In a long-term study begun in the 1960s, only 4% of "easygoing" lawyers died before age fifty. Twenty percent of lawyers who ranked in the top quarter of hostility scores on a survey assessing Type A personality died before age fifty. Of course, we have to be careful with a study that finds "easygoing" lawyers. I didn't think there was such a creature.

This risk of premature death has been corroborated in other research. Insurance companies send out surveys and keep tabs on age and mortality. Some of the early research was done by alumni associations. One of the things that's going to happen after you graduate from college is that our alumni association will send you appeals asking for donations. This will happen for the rest of your life. In this research alumni associations sent out surveys assessing who among their graduates were Type A personalities. Scores on these surveys were correlated with age at mortality. Who among the alumni were alive? Who have died? What was their age at death? The finding is clear. The higher the score on the Type A survey, especially on the hostility component, the greater the risk of dying at a younger age than norms anticipated for people of a particular age. Keep in mind that these are correlational studies. Without question, anger affects the cardio-vascular system, but another variable—perhaps a genetic variable—may be the causative factor in both the expression of anger and the state of the cardio-vascular system.

I'll like to introduce the concept of *catharsis*. This is the very old belief that expressing an emotion relieves or reduces the emotion. This concept of catharsis applies to every emotion, but we're speaking of it in the context of anger.

The concept of catharsis is tied in with literary criticism and it is a folk belief, too. We all know the belief that it's best not to hold anger in, because we'll stew in our juices and build the pressure up and explode. I saw that happen once. I was on 14th St. and Second Ave. and a man a half block ahead of me exploded. Simply exploded. I couldn't believe what I saw. I wasn't hurt and I didn't get pelted by body parts. I was in shape and limber in those days. His pancreas was flying toward me—I ducked to the right. His heart was flying toward me—I ducked to the left. His small intestines were slithering on the sidewalk like a sidewinder snake on sand—I leaped in the air and they swirled under me on the way to 13th St. Like I say, I was in good shape back then—I've since let myself go. If someone exploded in front of me nowadays, I'd have to stop at the dry cleaner's.

A police officer rushed up and asked, "What happened here?" I answered, "I don't know, officer, but that man exploded. I don't think he split his sides laughing. He must have been holding anger in for too long."

Like so many beliefs, catharsis is wrong. When it comes to anger we might say dead wrong. Expressing an emotion does not reduce the emotion. *Expressing an emotion increases the emotion.* Expressing anger does not reduce anger. Expressing anger increases anger.

I might clarify this and say that expressing anger would reduce anger if the expression was justifiable and directed only at the situation that provoked it. But it rarely works that way. When we get angry, we lose our composure and blow our tops—not enough to explode, but some of us get close enough.

Consider an example. Your spouse says something that disrespects you. "You're sloppy." "You're lazy." "You're dirty." "You don't make enough money." You get angry and you promptly disrespect your spouse, who immediately becomes angry. "You can't cook." "You're a gossip." "You're cheap." "You spend my money wastefully." As Harry

Stack Sullivan pointed out, the easiest way to recover our self-esteem is to lower it in another person.

Our voices rise. We turn red. We gesture animatedly. We start to argue. We drift into a topic we covered in the memory lecture—*mood-congruent retrieval*. We remember all the times our spouses disrespected us in the past. We remember all the times we became angry. Our spouse also experiences mood-congruent retrieval. Our spouse remembers all the times we disrespected him or her. Our spouse remembers all the times we made him or her angry. Before we know it, we're arguing at cross purposes and about different topics. I'm arguing about topic X. My spouse is arguing about topic Y. Neither topic has any relation to the original provocation Z.

There's another reason why catharsis is wrong and why the expression of anger increases anger, but you'll have to wait a few minutes to find it out.

What can be done when we become angry? We can step away from the situation. We can step out of the room. We can go outside and sit on the stoop. We can take a walk around the block. We can go to the store. Most emotions, anger included, are transitory. Think about happiness. If we hear a joke in the morning, we don't laugh all day long. We laugh for a moment and then move on. It's the same with anger. If we step away, we should be able to calm down. We're not going to find ourselves splattered across the sidewalk. Our insides are not going to inspire middle-aged men to perform acrobatics. By staying calm or by becoming calm, we maintain control of the situation. We may be able to focus on the original provocation. We may even make our spouses more angry. When a person is angry, there's nothing more maddening than to see the other person in an argument stay calm and in control of his or her emotions.

Of course, if we're the kind of person who gets angry in the morning and stays angry all day long, we need to consult a physician and get a prescription for a tranquilizer.

Let's move onto the emotion of *happiness*. If I do my job right, you should become unhappy.

Happiness is caused by acceptance and by increased self-esteem. The person thinks "acceptance" and moves to increase contact with others. The effect of happiness is affiliation. Nonverbally, the brow lowers. The eyes brighten. Gazing increases. There may be a smile and laughter. Speech is rapid and inflected upward. There is a slight increase in heart rate and an increase in limb temperature.

Happiness inspires us to make contact with others. When we become happy we want to reach out to others and get them to share in the happiness. We laugh to make connections with others. In conversations speakers laugh more than listeners. Laughter tells the other person that I am not offensive. I'm don't mean you harm. We laugh mostly at things that are not funny—this happens to me whenever I try to tell a joke.

Anger kills. Laughter has the opposite effect. There's an old saying, "He who laughs, lasts." Unlike most old sayings, this one seems to be true. Vigorous laughter is an aerobic exercise. Laughter increases breathing and circulation. Laughing two hundred times a day is comparable to rowing for ten minutes. Laughter reduces stress hormones and lowers blood pressure. These effects help the immune system to function better. On a *Star Trek The Next Generation* episode there was a character who practiced laughing for an hour a day. That's fiction, but it may be a practice we should emulate in the nonfiction world. For an hour at least the anger will be kept at bay.

There is no single source of happiness and there are no general guides to happiness, despite the many theories and gurus on the subject. George Orwell wrote that we can "Never be happy if we make happiness our goal." Happiness has to derive from the routine tasks of our lives. Happiness is a by-product of the everyday experiences of living. Many people make happiness their objective. These people would be happier if they made something else their objective.

Happiness is not related to gender. Women are no happier than men and vice versa. Happiness is not related to marriage or to parenthood. Married people are no happier than single people. Happiness is not related to appearance. Good-looking people are no happier than appearance-challenged people. Happiness is not related to a religious outlook. Pious people are no happier than atheists. Happiness is not related to wealth or to affluence. To a point, adding more money to our income does not increase happiness.

I'll like to dwell on the last point because many people believe they would be happy—more happy—if they became wealthy. This is not necessarily true. There has been a growth in affluence in the industrialized world in the past fifty years, but there has been no increase in overall happiness. Surveys that correlate happiness and affluence find no increase in happiness when affluence increases. Two or more generations of Americans have experienced large increases in wealth and there has been no appreciable change in reported happiness. Beyond a certain minimum level of income, happiness does not increase. I'm not sure this level can be defined with finality, but it appears to be surprisingly low. The figures I've seen are an income around $20,000 - $50,000.

There are a number of reasons why increasing wealth does not necessarily increase happiness. Material goods increase in the same proportion as income. There are a lot more objects to buy. As affluence increases, so does the desire to obtain goods. We can never have enough, because there is always something new to buy.

As material goods increase, we start to live stressful lives. We spend more time working in order to buy things. We spend more time commuting. We may have a lot of disposable income, but we have to work very hard in order to maintain our lifestyle.

Material goods do not address all human needs. There's another old saying that appears to be true—"The best things in life aren't things." There is love and affection and companionship and creativity. Money can't buy these. And it is those things that truly make us happy.

In a consumer society like ours the assumption is that increasing alternatives and offering customers increased choices increase happiness. In fact, the opposite may be true. Think of the bookstore. So many titles to choose from. Think of the supermarket. So many products to select. Think of the eyeglass store. There are so many frames for sale we spend hours trying to pick one we like. Think of the Internet. Think of cable television. Think of the sandwich shop. Ordering a sandwich is now a stressful experience because of all the choices we have to make. We have far more choices than previous generations, but we are no happier. We have so many choices, we can't make up our minds.

It happened to me just the other day that I drove into a nearly empty parking lot. I didn't know which space to park in. Maybe I should take this spot—no, it's too dim here. Maybe I should take this spot—no, it's too nearly a curve. Maybe I should take this spot—no, it's too isolated. I drove around for fifteen minutes before making up my mind where to park. You can be sure if I drove into a lot with a single space left, I would have taken it. And I would have felt very happy to get it.

We have so many choices, but we're no happier. We can never be sure we made the right choice. The more choices we have, the more disappointments, regrets, and second thoughts we'll have. I worried all day long whether I picked the right parking space. In our consumer-driven society we can never be sure we've weighed all the alternatives. We can never be sure of the alternatives. We're at the mercy of the media, after all, and of the people who build the products we buy. Don't forget, the guy who welded the rivets on the hull of the *Titanic* was having a bad day and taking shortcuts. In a technological society in which products are incessantly changing, our choice is sure to be obsolete in a short period. There's always something new and improved coming on the market and we just spent our paycheck on yesterday's model.

There are two phenomena that concern happiness and make us regard happiness in a slightly different light. The first is adaptation level. The second is relative deprivation.

Adaptation level is the phenomenon in which *we interpret our current happiness in the light of our past level of happiness.*

For example, a student receives a grade of B+ on the second quiz. The resultant happiness depends on what the student received on the first quiz. A grade of B+ results in happiness if the previous grade was C+. A grade of B+ does not result in happiness if the previous grade was A.

Consider the following. This year you get a raise of fifty cents an hour. Your happiness over this raise depends on what you received last year. If you got a raise of twenty five cents last year, you probably feel happy. Things are looking up. But you don't feel happy if you got a raise of seventy five cents last year. Things are looking down.

The principle of the adaptation level can lead to some odd comparisons. Maurice Greenberg was a financier and capitalist. He was the creative power behind the American International Insurance Co. that was one of the corporations that was deemed "too big to fail" in the great recession of 2008. He was also a majority stockholder. He was interviewed after the stock market crashed and the government bailed out American International. The interviewer asked how much his stock was worth before the market crashed. The figure was something like two hundred million. The interviewer then asked how much the stock was worth after the market crashed. The figure was something like sixty million. He didn't know it, but Maurice Greenberg expressed the adaptation level phenomenon at this moment in the interview. He commented that his sixty million dollars of stock was "virtually worthless." When I heard his comment I also suffered the adaptation level phenomenon. If I had sixty million dollars of stock, I'd take baths in which fifty dollar bills serve as bubbles.

Relative deprivation is the phenomenon in which *we interpret our current state of happiness in comparison to the condition and happiness of other people.* Our current happiness depends on what other people have and do. This is an easy concept to remember. Our judgment is relative—and our comparison is to our relatives. We don't compare our state to that of financiers and capitalists. We compare our state to the people we know—to our siblings, our in-laws, and our friends.

So a student receives a grade of B+ on the quiz. This student feels happy until he finds out that everyone else in the class got A's. This student will feel quite happy if he finds out that everyone else in the class got grades of B-. You get a raise of fifty cents an hour. You feel happy until you discover all your co-workers got raises of seventy five cents. You won't feel happy at all. Of course, you'll feel ecstatic if you discover that your co-workers got raises of twenty five cents.

The relative deprivation phenomenon may contribute to why multiplying choices makes us unhappy. We have more money and there are more things to buy. But our relatives have something we don't. They have a DVD player that peels apples. Our DVD player only plays movies. We have to peel apples the old-fashioned way. We don't feel happy. We not only have to buy a new DVD player, we have to buy apples.

There are so many things to buy. There are so many innovations. There are so many technological improvements. We need second jobs just to keep up. He didn't know he referred to the relative deprivation phenomenon, but the comedian Lewis Black offered this observation— in the old days people had to keep up with the Joneses. Today, people have to keep up with the Sun King, Louis XIV.

I'll like now to describe the James-Lange theory of emotion, which has been the most influential theory of emotion. The theory is named for William James and Carl Lange. James was a prominent philosopher and writer. He was one of the founders of American psychology. Carl Lange was a Dane, which is reason to be suspicious. I'm sure he was a fine man, but I don't know anything else about him I'm embarrassed to say. Both men independently published the same theory of emotion in the 1880s, which is why we have two names attached to one theory.

If you never heard of the James-Lange theory of emotion, I have the thrill of introducing it to you. The theory has three steps. *The first step is something happens.* We hear a joke. We get bad news in the mail. Someone pulls out a switchblade in the tavern. *The second step is the reaction of the autonomic nervous system.* The nerves in our *viscera* respond. By the viscera I mean the organs inside our chests and bellies. *In the third step we become aware of how our viscera is responding.* The third step involves the experience of emotion. *We have an emotion as we become aware of the response of the viscera.*

The James-Lange theory gives primacy to the body and to the autonomic nervous system. Cognition—awareness of the emotion—comes after the body responds. Other viewpoints suggest the opposite. Cognition comes first and then the autonomic nervous system responds. But James-Lange most definitely claimed that changes in the viscera occur *before* we experience emotion and cognition.

One implication of their claim is clear. If we do not become aware of the autonomic response of the viscera, then we do not have an emotion. The heart may be racing, the lungs may be huffing and puffing, and the intestines may be twisting themselves into knots, but if we do not become aware of this activity, then we do not have an emotion.

I saw this happen one time on the Fordham campus. I had a buddy named Joe—I'm not going to say his family name, because you may know him. I don't know who you know and it's not proper to use buddies as examples in psychology lectures. In any event, Joe was having difficulty with a teacher. He had an appointment with this teacher and came out of the meeting incensed about something the teacher said. He was red in the face and on the top of his head—I know he was red on the top of his head because he was bald. He was so irate he used swearwords—you're not supposed to use swearwords on a Catholic campus. I mentioned to him that he was angry, ferociously angry. Joe screamed at me, "I'm not angry!" I believed him. I told him that I was observing the failure of the third step in the James-Lange theory of emotion. He screamed back at me, foaming at the lips, "I am not an example of the failure of the third step in the James-Lange theory of emotion!" I didn't believe him.

There's another implication in the James-Lange theory that follows from giving the body primacy. Most people—certainly, the people who live in the Red Hook neighborhood of Brooklyn—believe that first we feel happy and then we laugh, and first we feel sad and then we cry, and first we feel fear and then we run. The James-Lange theory turns these viewpoints in reverse. The James-Lange theory suggests that first we laugh and then we feel happy, and first we cry and then we feel sad, and first we run and then we feel fear.

It may be that the original statements are also correct and that the people who live in the Red Hook section of Brooklyn know what they're talking about. It could be that both categories of statements are true and that how and when we feel emotion depends on the context. There may be occasions when we become happy only after we laugh, as James-Lange suggest. And there may be occasions when we feel happy and start to laugh. And there may be occasions when we start to laugh and feel happier. The latter is a distinct possibility, as you'll hear in a few moments.

The James-Lange theory is interesting, since it makes us think of emotions differently. It was the dominant theory in the study of emotion for some thirty and more years. The theory came under fire from two other researchers, Walter Cannon and Philip Bard. Walter Cannon, as you remember from the lecture on motivation, was a famous physiologist and author. I don't know anything about Philip Bard other than he was a not-so-famous physiologist and author. I'm sure he was a fine man and devoted to his family, but that's all I know. I realize it isn't much and I apologize.

Cannon-Bard criticized the James-Lange theory by suggesting the viscera was too slow and too diffuse of nerve power to account for the diversity and for the immediacy of emotions. When we hear a joke, we laugh immediately. When we get bad news, we cry immediately. When someone pulls out a switchblade in the tavern, we push our date forward and immediately race to the exit. The autonomic nervous system reacts too slowly for the immediacy of our emotional responses.

Cannon-Bard suggested the experience of emotions involved a dual process. The autonomic nervous system responds and the situation is evaluated by the central nervous system. This evaluation is immediate and doesn't depend on changes in the viscera. Cannon-Bard guessed the thalamus was responsible for emotion, but they guessed wrongly. As you recollect from the lecture on the brain and behavior, the thalamus connects the peripheral nervous system with the cerebral cortex.

For some forty years the James-Lange theory laid in its tomb after being knocked out of the textbooks by Cannon-Bard. Like the good theory it was, it returned from the dead in the 1970s and continues to guide research. It's my thrill to introduce the new and improved James-Lange theory. It remains a three-step process.

The first step is something happens. We hear a joke. We get bad news in the mail. Someone pulls out a switchblade in the tavern. In the second step the autonomic nervous system responds. But it's not the viscera. It's the *face* that responds. The third step is the same. We have an emotion as we become aware of what our face is doing.

The implications of the theory remain the same. We have an emotion only as we become aware of changes in the face. If we're not aware of facial changes, we don't have an emotion. As in the original version of the theory, bodily changes—in this case, changes in the face—precede the experience of emotion.

The viscera is slow and—forgive me—stupid. The face is superbly equipped with nerves and with blood vessels. And the face has forty three muscles with which to express the intricacies of emotion. That makes the face rather smart.

The face may not be the origin of emotion—the origin is a far more complex and multi-layered place. But the face provides *feedback* in the overall experience of emotion and the face certainly *modulates* emotion.

If we want to experience or to intensify an emotion, we "put on the face." If we want to experience happiness, we make a happy face. If we want to experience sadness, we make a sad face. If we want to experience fear, we make the fear face. Actors are taught these techniques in acting school. Children know these things without attending acting school. We have only to watch children as they experience an emotion or want to experience an emotion.

If we want to become angry or to stay angry, we make the angry face. Making the angry face, we get angrier. This is another reason why catharsis is wrong. Putting on the angry face doesn't relieve anger, it intensifies anger.

Facial expression of an emotion intensifies the emotion. Preventing or short-circuiting facial expression of an emotion reduces that emotion.

So the big boss returns from lunch with a mustard stain on his shirt. I want to laugh, but my review is coming up and the economic situation is not promising. If I start to laugh I'll lose control. I bite my lip so I can't laugh. I go to the wake of a good friend. I feel very sad. My lips start to tremble. Tears start to flow. But I'm a man. I have a reputation to uphold. If I start to cry I'll lose control and bawl like the paid keeners in the rear pews. I bite my lip so I can't make the sad face. I'm at the tavern. Someone flashes a switchblade. I'm terrified, but I don't want to bolt for the door and look unmanly in front of the ladies. Not to mention in front of the gentlemen. I bite my lip so I can't make the fear face. If anyone asks about that banging noise, I'll say it's not my knees but the pipes under the floorboards. That's a lie, but they don't know it.

Modern psychology suggests that we are *two faced*. Our faces tell other people what we're feeling. At the club tonight we see a person with an angry face or with a fear face. This face tells us, "Stay away. I'm not pleasant. I'm not okay. Leave me alone. I'm going to bite." We see another person with a happy face or with a face expressing interest. This face tells us, "Approach. I'm pleasant. I'm okay. I'm available. I'm not going to bite."

Our faces also tell ourselves how we feel. They tell the little men in our heads our current emotional states—if you're female, you can write little women, but I think someone already has. Feedback from the face may result from autonomic processes involving muscles, blood flow and temperature, and from the self-awareness that "I am feeling such-and-such an emotion at this moment." Experiencing an emotion causes us to make a face. Making a face causes us to experience the emotion more intensely.

As I mentioned at the outset of the lecture, the study of nonverbal expression was one of the hottest topics in psychology in the 1970s and 1980s. A lot of the research involved the videotape machine. We could film the face in interactions. We could play the recording in slow motion. We could stop the recording. We could watch it over and over. This development was an example of a relatively cheap technology opening up a field of research and enhancing our knowledge. The camcorder became the Hubble telescope of the study of emotion.

There were a lot of clever experiments at the time. The problem in doing research involving emotions was experimenters had to get people to make facial expressions without telling them. If experimenters told participants they were studying a particular emotion, this could bias the result. Since emotions can be posed and faked, people could make the face without feeling the emotion. Let me tell you about one such experiment. It might make you into a happier person.

Strack and others in 1988 randomly selected their participants to form three groups. One group held a pen in their front teeth. The second group held a pen loosely in their lips without using their teeth. The third group held the pen in their non-dominant hands—this group served as the control group. All three groups watched cartoons of the *Tom and Jerry* variety. After the cartoons they were asked a number of questions about the cartoons, including how funny they rated the cartoons on a one-to-nine scale of funniness.

Participants in the group that held the pen in their front teeth rated the cartoons funniest (the group average was 5.14). Participants in the group that held the pen in their lips without using the teeth rated the cartoons as least funny (the group average was 4.32). Participants in the group that held the pen in their hands rated the cartoons at an intermediate level (the group average was 4.77).

Strack and his colleagues suggested that holding the pen in the front teeth stimulated the muscles in the corners of the mouth that are involved in smiling and laughing. Stimulating these muscles—without telling the participants to smile or laugh—intensified the feeling of happiness. Hence, the higher rating on the survey. Holding the pen in the lips dampened the smile and might even have instigated a pout. Holding the pen in the hand had no influence on facial expression, obviously, and may have served as a baseline of the cartoon's funniness.

There are a few objections to this study. The differences between the averages of the groups, while statistically significant (the difference was beyond chance, given a certain risk of drawing the wrong conclusion), are small—one rating point. It would have been more impressive if the difference was three or four ratings points. We might further object that holding an object in the teeth or in the lips is a disagreeable task. The experimenters entertained this possibility. They asked both experimental groups to rate how difficult it was to hold the pen. There was no difference in average difficulty between participants who held the pen in their lips or in their teeth.

A final point about the experiment. The experimenters used a degree of deception in order not to disclose the purpose of the experiment.

They told the participants that the purpose of the experiment was to investigate psychomotor coordination. To pull off the ruse, they included a number of other tasks in the procedure, such as having the participants draw lines. Deception is always a controversial topic in experiments. We shall face the issue of deception again in a much more famous context in the lecture on social psychology.

If you are impressed by this one-point difference between groups, the implication is clear. If you want to go through life in a happy state, keep a pen gripped in the front teeth. If you are unimpressed by this one-point difference, you'll have to search for the source of happiness someplace else.

Thank you.

Tips to Students ~
Listening as a Skill

Listening is more than the passive reception of sound. Listening is an active process in which we pay attention to what a person is saying. Listening is a skill that requires concentration and engagement. It is a complex task that cannot be performed while other cognitive tasks are going on.

Here are some pointers on how to listen.

Listen—*do not do anything else while listening*. It is flattering to a person for you to devote your undivided attention to what he or she has to say. It is disrespectful to do something else while another person is speaking.

Do not interrupt. It is disrespectful to interrupt when a person is talking. Wait for the person to finish to make a reply. When you interrupt you may not hear the complete statement a person wants to make.

Block out distracting thoughts while you listen—including thoughts about what you are going to say in reply. We cannot simultaneously listen and formulate our replies.

It is not necessary to give a profound or witty answer when the person is done speaking. In most cases it is not necessary to listen with a critical attitude.

Try to follow the theme or gist of what the person is saying. It is useful to repeat back to the person the theme or gist of what he or she said. This can be done by summarizing what the person said or by responding to it in a manner that shows you understood what was said. Sometimes this can be done by repeating back to the person *in other words*—in your own words—what was said.

If you are not clear what a person said, you can say so explicitly or you can ask questions in order to obtain clarification. Of course, you should ask for clarification in a nice way.

LECTURE FOUR ~
Health Psychology and Stress

Health psychology is the subfield or specialty that applies the principles of psychology to the issues of sickness and wellness. It's currently a popular subfield, as you might imagine. Americans want to avoid getting sick. If we get sick, we want to recover expeditiously. If we can help it, we want to avoid dying. And we want to look good, no matter how good or bad the state of our health.

An objective of health psychology is to prevent people from getting sick. Probably, there's an element of inevitability about getting sick. We have categorical predispositions to contend with. These predispositions include genetics and an element of chance and luck in experiencing a particular social-cultural milieu. Think, for example, how antibiotics and sanitation have improved our chances. Because of the happenstance of the time in which we live, we don't die of sicknesses that claimed our ancestors at young ages. And we don't experience infectious diseases due to poor sewerage and contaminated water supplies. At least we don't in the industrialized world.

Beyond these biological and social-cultural elements there are aspects of our lifestyles that make us sick. Think of the lives lost yearly to tobacco and to poor diet and to alcohol and to substance abuse and to unprotected sex and to reckless driving and to murder and to suicide. The numbers are staggering—it's estimated that a million American lives a year are lost to the abusive lifestyles I mentioned. There's nothing biological about these aspects of lifestyle. There's nothing genetic about them. Lifestyle is determined by culture and by learning. It may be difficult, but we can alter our lifestyles. If we don't smoke and consume junk food and alcohol and shoot up illegal substances and if we don't have unprotected sex and if we drive carefully and if we avoid getting murdered or murdering ourselves, we would never die.

Health psychology also tries to get us to feel better and to recover our health if we lose it. It aims to use the principles of psychology to treat sicknesses. And it aims to get people to comply with the doctor's orders and to take their medications properly. A substantial number of people do not take medicine as prescribed, even in serious illnesses. And health psychology aims to move people toward the state of *wellness*.

Wellness is a positive and dynamic state of health. It is a place beyond simply not being sick—I think it's located between Sweden and Lithuania. Simply not being sick at a particular moment is not the same as being well. We may not have a particular illness, but we may not be in the pink of health. Consider myself. I'm not sick at this moment. I don't have a particular disease—if I have one, I don't want to know about it—but I can't say I'm a citizen of the state of wellness. I'm not sick, but I'm not in peak condition. I was a few years ago, but I'm ashamed to say I let myself go. If I want to become a citizen of wellness, I'd have to get my passport in order—I wouldn't want to get in trouble with the border patrol. I'd have to work out and eat better and change my attitudes and stop carousing all hours of the night in cheap gin mills located near the docks.

One of the main concepts in health psychology is *stress*, which is defined as the *physiological and psychological responses to the demands life makes on us*. Stress is something we moderns are under. Stress is ubiquitous. Stress can make us sick. If we're sick, stress can make us sicker. If we're not sick, but not in the greatest shape, stress can keep us from crossing the border into the bright sunshiny world of wellness.

We call stress by many different words. We call stress "worry" when we're preoccupied with the cares and toils of life. (There's a common expression that a person is "sick with worry.") We call stress "fear" when we face a medical procedure. We call stress "anxiety" and "stage fright" when we have to present a proposal at work. We call stress "depression" when our company downsizes and we find ourselves unemployed. We call stress "frustration" when the train breaks down on the way to class. We call stress "shame" and "guilt" when we have an argument with the spouse and use bad words and tear down his or her self-esteem.

There was a concept some years ago called *eu-stress*. This was the idea that certain types of stress-inducing experiences could propel us into the state of wellness. These experiences included jogging, weight lifting, and strenuous workouts. There may be an element of truth in the concept that stress can be adaptive if the exercises were performed correctly and if everything else in our lives ran smoothly. There was also an element of danger in these exercises for a reason I'll mention shortly. I'll like to suggest that all stress amounts to *dis-stress* and that all stress, regardless of its origin, can affect us in harmful ways.

Stress is caused by *stressors*. Stressors are what lead to stress. How's that for a circular definition? There are three major categories or sources of stressors. These categories are daily hassles, life changes, and catastrophes.

The most common category of stressor involves *daily hassles*. Consider a ride on the uptown IRT. The car is crowded, noisy and dangerous. Someone is talking too loud. Someone else smells. Someone else is staring at you coldly. You get off the train and the traffic is heavy. Who's running a red light? Who's speeding up as you step off the sidewalk to jaywalk? You get to school. There's a line in the cafeteria. The escalators are broken. The elevators are down. The professor is dull. You hear an announcement about a quiz you didn't know what coming.

Living in cities such as New York can be exciting—after all, if we can't make it here, where can we make it? There's more money in cities and more health care, but living in cities is inherently stressful. There's more noise in cities, more pollution, more social pressure, and more competition—we scrape to get ahead in the corporate world and we scamper to get that seat on the train ahead of the slower passengers. There are fewer community ties in cities and more social isolation. Many people are alone in the crowd and by themselves in the metropolis—that doesn't sound like a good place to be.

Daily hassles are the ubiquitous annoyances and vexations we face on a routine basis. They are the inconveniences we suffer for being civilized. Let me mention two—noise and information overload.

Cities are noisy places and noise is stressful. Noise is also unhealthy, as it produces hearing loss and other negative changes in physiology. Noise comes from many sources—crowded apartments, television sets, sports events and concerts, traffic and trains, and from the flight paths of planes. Studies done on changes to the Munich airport in the early 2000s found that noise is positively correlated with higher blood pressure, with increased levels of stress hormones, and with problems in reading comprehension in children. Noise may even disrupt long-term memory.

In a classic study done in the 1970s Arline Bronzaft found that the classroom performance and cognitive functioning of children were affected by how noisy their neighborhood was. Children whose windows bordered elevated train tracks were a year behind children whose windows were on the other side of the apartment building and away from the noise of the trains. Elevated train tracks are mostly gone from your country of New York, which is a good thing. (When I started at Fordham decades ago, they were tearing down the elevated tracks that ran along Third Ave. in the Bronx. The noise of trains was replaced by the quieter BX 55 bus.) But noise is still with us. Noise is the number one quality of life complaint in New York City.

Each of us has to deal with information overload. In 1997 a book by David Shenk was published called *Data Smog*. Shenk suggested we were drowning in a tsunami of information. The author did not think this was a good thing. We have too much data to consider over the most trivial topic. We are being pulled under by a sea of words and numbers. We are going under and we can't help ourselves. We can't stop. We certainly can't stop to think.

I don't have to tell you the situation has grown worse since Shenk published the book. Information has become smoggier and we are more than ever affected by stress. We have the world at our fingertips via cell phones and hand-held computer gizmos. We can find anything out, anytime, anywhere. I suppose that's a good thing, but we pay a price. We have no chance to catch our breaths. We have no chance to think. We have no chance to evaluate matters. We can be reached anytime by anyone. We're frazzled. We fret constantly. Our nerves are shot.

I was at the bookstore recently. The assistant manager was taking my order. He didn't stop checking the computer screen. He was reading as I was speaking. The portable phone he carried on his belt rang. He answered it and conducted two conversations at the same time. A chiming sound came on the store's loudspeaker and "Austin" was instructed to go to the cash wrap. Austin took his eyes off the computer screen for the first time. He was sorely tempted to drop everything and proceed to the registers. The phone on his desk started to ring. I told him if he answered the phone I would pull out the pistol I carry in my valise and clip him—this is Mafia talk for getting shot in the knee cap. Austin looked surprised. He took his hand off the receiver. He gulped and smiled meekly. He thought I was joking. I wasn't. I felt sorry for him, deluged as he was in the smog of customer service. I felt sorry for myself. All I wanted to do was place one book order and I was suffocating in the smog that enveloped Austin's work station.

The second category of stressors involves *life changes*. Any *negative change* in our lives can increase stress. We get divorced. We get laid off. We lose our lease on the apartment. We get sick. We go broke. Our pet dog runs away. A relative dies.

It's clear that a negative event can rattle us and induce stress. It's important to note that *positive life changes* can also increase stress. Positive changes in our lives can be as intimidating as negative changes. We get married—we have to plan years ahead for the happy day when we live with another person. We get promoted—we have to work longer hours and hire and fire people. We get an apartment—we have to buy furniture and deal with noisy neighbors. A baby is born—we have to get up all hours of the night to feed the baby. We adopt a new pet that has to be housebroken. We come into money—we have to hire accountants to hide our money from the IRS and we find out that we have relatives we never knew existed.

The third and rarest category of stressors in the industrialized world is *catastrophes*. These are serious events, usually unpredicted, that affect a lot of people at once and make enormous demands on us. Catastrophes are so serious they may be said to change our lives all at once and in ways we may not be prepared for. A fire guts a tenement. A deranged person shoots up a classroom. A flood destroys a community. A tornado rips through a town. A hurricane washes the coast away. A plane crashes into the bay. Planes crash into skyscrapers.

We are sensitive today to the psychological dislocations caused by catastrophes. Trained counselors assist in helping survivors handle the trauma and the grief. This is a relatively new process. Before the 1970s people were pretty much left on their own to manage the effects of catastrophes. There was always some regard of the public and physical damage wrought by catastrophes. That's what insurance was for. But it was only recently that there was a regard for the psychological effects of catastrophes. These might be said to be the private effects. People tried not to show them. People tried not to notice them.

One of the first investigations of the psychological effects of catastrophes was done on the survivors of the Buffalo Creek, West Virginia, flood. Early in the morning of Feb. 26, 1972 a dam broke, releasing a wall of water twenty feet high that swamped a town in Buffalo Creek Valley. The flood destroyed nearly every home in the valley. Four thousand people were left homeless. One hundred twenty five died. The survivors were relocated into trailer homes near the valley. Two years passed before they were allowed to return and restart their lives.

Kai Erickson interviewed survivors of the flood and found serious psychological aftereffects—this is detailed in the 1976 book *Everything in Its Path—the Buffalo Creek Flood*. Survivors experienced disruption and dislocation. Their worldviews were shaken and altered. Religious people suffered a loss of connection with their faith. "Why has God done this to us?" they asked and "Why have evil people survived and good people died?" Erickson found that survivors had difficulty concentrating. They had increased anxieties and fears. They felt guilty for surviving. They blamed themselves for failing to do more. Children regressed. Survivors exhibited phobias for events that preceded the flood. They became afraid of rain and of darkness. They panicked when storms broke out. They had trouble sleeping and experienced nightmares. They slept in their clothes to be ready to outrun the next flood.

We understand these behaviors as characteristic of post-traumatic stress disorder. They might be called the "normal" or "routine" response to experiencing a catastrophe. (As we shall see in the lecture on psychological disorders, post-traumatic stress disorder follows the occurrence of traumatic events.) The reactions of the people of Manhattan who experienced the attack on the Twin Towers were similar to the people of Buffalo Creek Valley.

Terrorism presents a new source of stress for Americans. Formerly, we didn't have to worry about planes crashing into buildings or about poisonous mail or about bombs going off at marathons. Now, we do. PATH trains have posters encouraging commuters to report suspicious activity and unattended bags. A radio commercial advises that "We're all on the frontline against terror." Television and social media present the aftermath of terror instantaneously. People geographically distant from a terrorist strike experience it as if they were present.

The relation of stressors, whether experienced individually or collectively, and post-traumatic stress disorder has serious health implications. A very large study of more than two hundred thousand veterans in California and Nevada commenced in 2009. All the veterans were free of heart disease and diabetes at the outset of the study. Some, but not all, were diagnosed with post-traumatic stress disorder. They were followed for the next three years. (They are still being followed). By 2012 35% of the veterans who were diagnosed with post-traumatic stress disorder developed insulin resistance compared with 19% of the veterans who had not been diagnosed with post-traumatic stress disorder. Insulin resistance is a precursor condition to diabetes. In addition, 53% of veterans diagnosed with post-traumatic stress disorder exhibited metabolic syndrome compared with 37% of veterans who had not been diagnosed. Metabolic syndrome involves a dangerous combination of high body fat, high cholesterol, high blood pressure, and high blood sugar.

Regardless of the source of the stress—daily hassles, life changes, and catastrophes—the effect of stress is *cumulative. Accumulative*, we might say. We experience financial stressors, health stressors, weather stressors, transportation stressors, relationship stressors, work and career stressors, academic stressors—the various sources of stress load our bodies with tensions and with harmful chemicals. We say we're *stressed out*—the better phrase is *stressed in*. It's like loading a bag with stones. It doesn't matter what kind of stone or what quarry the stones come from. Put too many stones in and the bag is going to rip.

The cumulative effect of stress is the reason why "eu-stress" may not be such a good thing. Eu-stress drops another stone in the bag.

I said stress loads our bodies with tensions and with chemicals and I wasn't kidding—I would never kid about a thing like this. A cascade of chemical events follows once stress is experienced. The hypothalamus releases corticotrophin-releasing hormone that activates the pituitary gland. The pituitary gland releases hormones that increase the level of glucose in the bloodstream. The pituitary also releases ACTH (adrenocorticoptrophic-releasing hormone). ACTH activates the adrenal glands to release epinephrine (adrenaline) from the medulla and cortisol from the cortex.

The sympathetic nervous system is aroused as well, triggering the fight-and-flight response. We're mobilized for action. That's not a bad thing in and of itself. We need a jolt every once in a while. If we don't get a jolt by nearly getting run over or by nearly falling down a flight of stairs, we get it by riding upside-down roller coasters or by scuba diving with the sting rays. But the fight-and-flight response is not a good thing hour after hour, day after day, week after week. Our bodies break down. Our minds break down. We start to experience physical and psychological disorders.

I'll like now to review *person and situation variables* that affect stress, either relieving it or worsening it. These variables are individual differences in the appraisal and experience of stress, personality factors, the predictability of stress, social support, the interpretation of stress, coping mechanisms, socioeconomic issues, and the control or perceived control of the source of stress.

There are *individual differences* in the appraisal and experience of stress. Some differences may be learned. We do a better job after the second hurricane than we did after the first. We grow use to stress on the job. Some differences may be based on temperament. Some people are more active and assertive than others in grappling with the sources of stress. Other people just think about doing something and never get around to addressing the sources of stress.

There are differences in handling stress. Some people can handle a lot more stress before their bags tear. And there are different bags. Every person has a breaking point. Every person has a weakness. Some people get headaches when they're under stress. Other people get indigestion. Other people get rashes and skin conditions. Other people experience psychological maladies.

There may be *personality types* that handle stress differently. We've seen how the Type A personality acts—they're domineering, impatient, and hostile. They are constantly aroused and under stress. They're constantly fighting and fleeing.

There is a kind of personality or a kind of attitude or orientation that looks to be less affected by stress. This is the *optimistic personality*. Optimistic people appear to handle stress better. Like the Marines, they improvise, adapt, and overcome. They have stable and generalized positive expectations for their futures. They see the glass as half full rather than as half empty. They don't see problems, they see solutions that haven't happened yet.

The absence of rage and rancor may be beneficial to health. As it says in the *Book of Proverbs* (17:22), "A merry heart does good like a medicine." There is a large-scale study called "The Nun Study." An order of Catholic nuns in the Midwest dedicated their brains to science. The study is important because the nuns live virtuous lives. They don't drink, they don't smoke, they don't use swearwords. They are educated ladies who remain cognitively active throughout their lives. Many reach advanced ages.

The ostensible purpose of the research was to study Alzheimer's Disease. A subsidiary and surprising finding was the positive correlation between optimism and longevity. The nuns had to write autobiographical statements when they joined the convent. The researchers had access to these statements. They correlated the number of positive statements made when the women were young (in their late teens and early twenties) and the length of their lives. The nuns who wrote the most positive statements when they were young lived the longest.

The finding relating optimism to longevity and to good health has been found in other studies. In a forty year study conducted with University of North Carolina graduates pessimism was correlated with mortality—the most pessimistic individuals had nearly double the mortality rate than the most optimistic. In a study of three hundred nine coronary artery bypass surgery patients, optimism was associated with less troubled recoveries and with fewer incidents of re-hospitalization. In a study of two thousand five hundred people aged sixty five and older, optimism was negatively associated with high blood pressure. People with the most optimistic outlooks had the lowest blood pressure. In a study of thirteen hundred men over sixty years of age with no coronary artery disease, an optimistic outlook was negatively correlated with developing such disease over the next ten years. Men with the most pessimistic outlook were twice as likely to develop heart disease.

These findings are correlational, so they don't prove that optimism causes good health and long life, but they are suggestive. There may be a genetic link among these variables. Or there may be emotional and health issues of the kind we have been discussing. Optimistic people may be more adaptive and creative in solving problems. They may be less bothered by problems and less driven to solve them. They may be less frustrated, hence less affected by anger. The absence of an ever-present fight-and-flight response may be conducive to good health—the absence of epinephrine and cortisol continuously swirling through the arteries is beneficial. Optimistic people may make the happy face more than the sad face or the angry face and this may be beneficial. And they may laugh more.

I'll like to add that the beneficial effect of optimism appears to involve cardio-vascular diseases and no other kinds of disease. There is no positive correlation between optimism and the avoidance or successful treatment of cancer. Optimistic people suffering cancer do not survive longer than pessimistic people with cancer. And I'll like to add that the correlation between optimism and longevity found in the Nun Study has been questioned. The suggestion has been made that the nuns who lived the longest didn't express more optimism in their autobiographies than nuns who expressed less optimism. Rather, they wrote in an overly emotional style that included optimistic elements. Writing in a flowery style rather than in a dry matter-of-fact style would seem to have no obvious relationship to the length of one's life.

There are other factors that influence the severity of stress. One such factor is *predictability*. Is it possible to predict the onset and offset of stress? A collateral factor is whether we perceive stress as weakening or as worsening.

The unpredictable onset and offset of stress is worse than a predictable onset and offset. So is the judgment that stress is worsening.

Consider the chaotic world of retail. Salespeople know the onset of the Christmas stampede begins the day after Thanksgiving and ends the day after New Year's. That's bad enough. But it would be worse if the salespeople never knew when the Christmas season started. This sounds like a nonsensical example, but it's not farfetched. In many stores the Christmas season starts in September and ends—well, no one knows when it ends. The push nowadays is to keep the registers ringing all year round.

Consider allergies like hay fever. If we knew that we start to itch and sneeze at a particular time of year, we could prepare and load up with the antihistamines. Allergies would be worse if we never knew when they would strike.

The same is true of the course of a disease. If we knew that a disease or ailment would end by a particular time—or that we would end by a particular time—that would be stressful, but it would not be as bad as not knowing when we'd get well or when we'd take up the harp and strap on wings. If we foresee when stress ends—one way or another—we can prepare for it. If we don't foresee that stress ends—well, it's difficult to prepare for an open-ended and bad situation.

Another factor that affects the severity of stress is the *presence or absence of social support.* Stress is felt more keenly when there is no one to share it with. The malicious effects of stress are reduced when there are people to console us and comfort us and take our side and commiserate with us. Misery loves company—this is not a selfish thing. Misery loves company so tears of sorrow can transform into tears of joy. As the song goes, "Give me a shoulder to cry on." I'd make like Tony Bennett and sing the lyrics, only I can't carry a tune, which is a good thing for your ears.

When we are under stress and have people there for us, we reach out and get information. In business this is called "networking." In the health field this is called "a support group." We find out what to do. We find out that we're not alone. Other people have been there before us and faced the same problems. If we're lucky, they've solved the problems.

We reach out for a more basic reason—for the comfort of the human touch. Many years ago a psychologist named Harry Harlow did a famous experiment with rhesus monkeys. The experiment is usually covered in child psychology class, but it will serve us well now. Harlow separated baby monkeys from their mothers. He fed the monkeys using a wire-mesh "mother" who dispensed milk through a bottle. He also provided in the cage a wire-mesh "mother" dressed in terrycloth. This mother did not dispense milk—she just stood in place and did nothing. Harlow proceeded to frighten the monkeys unexpectedly to see which mother they would flee to. To everyone's surprise, they fled to the terrycloth mother and ignored the milk-dispensing mother. That's what we do when we are frightened or under duress—*dur-stress*, to coin a term. We reach out and hold on. Someone is there for us. Someone is for us. We feel comforted. We are not alone in this messed-up world. But to be alone and to have no one to hold onto—how bitter and painful that is. We're alone—how can we ever get well?

I might add that in religious circles healing comes about through the "laying on of hands." The suspicion is something supernatural is happening. But it may be something as ordinary as the feel of the human touch that inspires healing.

And I might add that Harlow's study with the baby monkeys has come under review. It was considered an important study at the time and it was frequently cited, but modern psychologists, who have a different moral sensibility, view the study as cruel and detrimental to members of a primate species.

Another factor that can weaken or worsen stress is whether we can *find a meaning* for the source of the stress. If we can find a meaning for the anguish we undergo, we understand the situation and it doesn't hurt so badly. Some people find a meaning for stressors in politics. "It's the reactionary Republicans." "It's the big-spending Democrats." "It's the selfish bourgeois class." "It's the greedy capitalists." Other people find a meaning for the stressors in science. "I shouldn't have eaten so much junk food." "I should have exercised more." "I should have had healthier ancestors." Other people find a meaning for the stressors in religion. These people see this world as a big schoolhouse and as a testing ground for the Hereafter. They see suffering as good for the soul. It even says in the Christian Bible (*Hebrews 12:6*), "Whom the Lord loves, he sends a lot of stressors to."

Stress hurts when we can't find a reason for its occurrence. "I voted and rated our politicians high. I watched my diet. I had quality ancestors. I performed the Corporal and Spiritual Works of Mercy. And look at all the stressors I face. It's not fair. It's not right." It's not a happy thought to realize that we did everything right and that we were done in by random bad luck.

Another factor that can worsen or weaken stress is the *cognitive coping skills* we bring to the situation. Other people may give us advice and some advice may be useful, but we may sabotage ourselves by our cognitive outlook and by our style of thinking.

Albert Ellis and Aaron Beck were two psychologists who favored a cognitive perspective. They believed stress worsened when people engaged in a *self-defeating cognitive style*. This style may involve *overgeneralization*. We predict that our problems and sources of stress will always occur. We get turned down after a job interview. We predict we will always be turned down. But we don't know that we will. We get rejected in love. We predict that we will always be rejected in love.

But we don't know that we will. Maybe our next job interview will go better. Maybe the next blind date will blossom into romance. The past does not have to be the future.

Another element in this self-defeating cognitive style is *over-personalization*. We touched on this as the "internal locus of control" in the personality lecture. This is the belief that we have complete control over our lives and the things that happen to us. We'll touch on a similar concept in the lecture on social psychology. This is the "fundamental attribution error," which is the tendency to look to personality for the causes of behavior and not to the situations people happen to be in. When we over-personalize we take things personally, too personally, highly personally. We take things to heart—we wear our hearts on our cuffs. We get rejected after the job interview. "It's not the economy. It's not the job opening. It's not the interviewer. *It's me.* I'm to blame. I'm at fault." When we over-personalize we think that we will always be unsuccessful. We get rejected in love. "It's not the other person. It's not the bad service or the poor cuisine in the fast-food restaurant I took her to. *It's me.* I'm not a lovable person." When we over-personalize we think that we will always be unloved and unlovable.

There's an element of a self-fulfilling prophecy in this faulty cognitive style. If we think we are going to be rejected in a job interview, we may look and act in such a way that guarantees rejection. And if we think we are going to be rejected in love, we may look and act in such a way that guarantees rejection. We become our own worse enemies. In spite of our best intentions, we fail. Stress marches on.

Ellis defined a number of faulty beliefs that make it difficult to solve the problems that result in stress. Since they are not possible to fulfill, these beliefs increase stress. Among such beliefs are the following. I must be liked by everyone. Everything must go my way. Everyone must approve what I say and do. I must be treated fairly. I must always be on top of my game. I must never make a mistake. I must always be perfect. I must never fail.

These beliefs complicate the situation and prevent us from solving our problems. We feel pressure from our own thoughts. We cannot be liked by everyone. Things don't always go our way. Life is not fair—I think President Jimmy Carter said this. Or it might have been the maintenance man in the Little League field. Recall that the effects of stress are cumulative. We're trying to solve our problems and these faulty beliefs clutter the mindscape. They are like weeds in a garden. We hate these beliefs, but we can't easily pull them out by the roots. We hate ourselves for thinking them.

Coping mechanisms involve the responses we make to stressful situations. How do we handle daily hassles? How do we meet the changes in our lives? How do we respond when traumatic events occur?

People differ in how they cope with stress. There are three general styles of coping. These styles are the active-behavioral style, the active-cognitive style, and the avoidant style.

People who exhibit the *active-behavioral style* cope with stress by taking an assertive stance. They try to do something to change the situation. They form a plan of action. They talk to people and try to get information. They do not hide their problems. They express their difficulties to other people.

People who exhibit the *active-cognitive style* cope with stress by thinking about various courses of action. They do not immediately take action. They review the situation. They ruminate. They speculate. They pray for guidance. They prepare for the worst. They are stuck in their thoughts and that seems a perilous place when stress assaults them.

People who exhibit the *avoidant style* prefer not to think about the sources of stress. It follows that they do not take action. They refuse to accept what is happening. They try to stay busy to keep their minds off the situation. They believe things will get better if they do not think about them. They hide their feelings and isolate themselves. They do not share or talk about their problems. They put their heads in the sand. Crabs bite their noses and stress marches on.

Another factor that affects stress is *socioeconomic status*. I don't have to tell you. I know it myself. Poverty and stress are best friends. Poverty and bad health are bosom buddies. The risk of some diseases increases ten times as we move down the socioeconomic ladder. There is as much as ten years difference in life expectancy between the highest and the lowest socioeconomic classes. This difference is true even when such factors as diet, health care, and housing are taken into consideration.

There are a number of obvious reasons for this discrepancy and there is one not so obvious reason. People in poverty experience more daily hassles than people higher on the socioeconomic ladder—remember the effects of stress are cumulative. People may have less access to health care or receive inferior care in emergency rooms. People in poverty may have poorer diets—a junk food diet is a path to obesity and to diabetes. People in poverty may have less access to information and to social networks. People in poverty may not have the right information. They may entertain the proverbial old wives' tales, some of which we've encountered on this intellectual voyage. Probably, this information comes from television sets—lower socioeconomic level children watch more television than higher socioeconomic level children. They may not know how to lift themselves out of poverty. They may think that it is not possible to better themselves. They may not be able to predict an end to stress.

There is an additional and less obvious factor that may be responsible for these differences between socioeconomic classes. This is the issue of *control* or *perceived control.* If we believe that we can control the sources of stress and that we can step out of the stressful situation at some point, stress doesn't sting as bad. If we believe that we have no control over the sources of stress and that we can never free ourselves of the stress, the sting is painful. People higher on the socioeconomic level can remove themselves from the stress. They can quit their jobs, they can seek different healthcare, they can put their money in a bank offering better terms, and so on. People in poverty are stuck. They're stuck in dead end jobs, they have no recourse in sickness than the physician on duty in the emergency room, they can't open a new account in a bank because they don't have enough funds.

Consider a study by Marmet and others conducted in England. They studied male civil servants over a ten-year period. Everyone from the top executives to the janitors had the same access to health care and the same health care plan. Despite this, the risk of heart disease and mortality from heart disease increased as one descended the corporate ranks. Chances of dying from heart disease were much greater for lower-level civil servants than for executives. Men in the lowest-level occupations had a threefold higher mortality rate than men in the highest-level occupations. One interpretation of this finding involves the issue of control. Lower-level employees had less control over their jobs and less job motility. They were stuck and couldn't move on. They didn't dare quit—they didn't have enough funds to tide them over and they didn't have friends in other companies to provide new jobs. They were in the position of receiving orders rather than in the position of giving orders. The executives told them where to go and when to get there. They couldn't tell the executives where to go.

A psychologist named Kobasa introduced the concept of *psychological hardiness*. (It's also called *resilience*.) A study of extremely active and harried business executives found the surprising outcome that they were not exhausted or stressed out—they weren't stressed in either. To the contrary, they were exhilarated. A closer examination found the following characteristics. The executives liked the challenges they faced and they were high in commitment. They saw challenges not as obstacles but as developments that could further their careers and businesses. Their jobs were their lives. They exhibited internal locus of control. They believed they could control events, unlike people in poverty or low-level civil servants.

Control is one thing. Some people have it. Some people lack it. The people who have no control should act *as if they have control*. This is referred to as *perceived control*. It makes a psychological difference if we act and try to influence the sources of stress rather than if we give up and do nothing.

Consider any social or political issue. We may be at the mercy of lobbyists and politicians. We may be at the beck and call of the high and mighty. We may think we can do nothing. We give up. Stress doesn't go away, it accumulates. We don't act, as the saying goes, because we don't know how much we can do. We can do something—we can do little somethings. We can write letters. We can send e-mails. We can call our representatives. We can march in parades and attend rallies. We can sign petitions. We can contribute pennies to candidates we like. We can put our two cents in. We can get it off our chests. We may understand our efforts may lead to nothing, but the mere act of doing something reduces stress.

I'll like to close by giving an example of perceived control from my life. When we started the Second Gulf War many years ago I wrote letters to George W. Bush and to Saddam Hussein. I addressed the former letter to the White House in Washington, DC. I addressed the latter to "Saddam Hussein. The Palace. Baghdad. Iraq." I wrote, "Dear President Hussein, it's recently come to my attention that war is imminent. Even as I write this, troops are massing on your borders. It's a sign of a leader that he knows when to fold the cards and get out of the game. It's the sign of a leader that he puts the interest of the citizens ahead of personal interests. I recommend that you put your millions in suitcases and proceed posthaste to the French Riviera where retired and ousted dictators spend their twilight years. Sincerely, Dennis Ford."

I was under no delusion that George W. Bush would call the troops back. And I was under no delusion that Saddam Hussein would read my letter and decide, "Boys, pack the bags, we're heading to the French Riviera." The letters weren't meant for them—I had no control over events. The letters were meant for me. They were written so that I could continue to have the vaguest, most fleeting, feeling of perceived control.

I recommend this technique of letter writing. It gives us a chance to review events and to organize our thinking on a topic. It gives us a chance to work through the emotions. And it allows us the perception that we have input and can control the sources of stress. This may not be entirely true. In fact, it's a lie—and we know we won't be caught. But lying is better than doing nothing, and that's something.

Thank you.

Tips to Students ~
Reviews, Daily and Major

Daily Reviews

Daily reviews include the notes you took on the daily reading of the textbook and the notes you took in the class lecture. Daily reviews would include material that has just been learned and material that requires memorization.

Before you begin today's reading review the notes you made yesterday. Doing so will build up continuity in the topic and provide repetition of the material.

Before you attend the next lecture review the notes you made during the previous lecture. This will help in highlighting material you may need the instructor to clarify and it will help to indicate confusions or gaps in the material.

Use your spare time—waiting for transportation, for example—to conduct daily reviews.

Major Reviews

Major reviews are conducted the week before quizzes. They should be longer than daily reviews, two or three hours at a stretch, during which you try to integrate concepts and acquire a deeper understanding of the material. These sessions should *not* be used to learn new material—that is the objective of daily study. These sessions should be used to elaborately rehearse material you already know.

During these sessions, study the most difficult subjects at the beginning of the study period.

Take breaks within the larger review period. Do not engage in intellectual activities during the breaks.

Reviewing is crucial to study and to learning, but it's all so easy to postpone reviewing.

Remember *repetition is the mother of memory*. The more you repeat something in an elaborative manner, the more likely you are to retrieve it when you need it.

LECTURE FIVE ~
Social Psychology

Perhaps you remember the lecture on personality. Personality theorists like Allport and Freud suggested that we are our personalities and that we possess traits like introversion and entities like the id, ego and superego. We are such things. They are us. In a fundamental manner we are our personalities. I am who I am, like it says in the Good Book. I is who I is, like Popeye says. This is true whether or not I eats me spinach.

Social psychologists suggest something different. They suggest that there is no unique and abiding personality inside us. Instead, we play many roles in the way an actor dons masks and becomes different characters. Social psychologists further suggest that we need to consider situations as important determinants of behavior. We can't study personality in glorious isolation. We have to study personalities—roles—as they occur in social situations.

Right now, I'm playing the role of a teacher. You are playing the roles of students. Later, I'll be playing the role of a customer in a particular store. Somebody will be playing the role of a salesperson. Still later, I'll be playing the role of a patron in my neighborhood tavern. Another person will be playing the role of a bartender. Tomorrow, I'll be playing the role of a penitent in church. Another person will be playing the role of a minister—he'll be admonishing me for my excesses in the tavern. There may be some commonality in all these roles, but observers would be surprised how differently I acted in each situation.

Personality theorists suggest that we act in a consistent manner, but social psychologists suggest that we act differently in different situations.

Social psychologists further suggest that we act differently when we are with other people than when we are alone. We act differently in groups and we act differently depending on the group we happen to be in. This is the bane of many parents. "My son is a good kid," parents say, "but he runs with a bad crowd and acts differently when he's with them." Social psychologists find this imminently possible.

The children acted differently in the bad group they fell in with, but there is no underlying personality that got subverted. In social psychology the operative idea is that we assume roles as we enter and exit particular groups. The personality changes in each group. The personality changes as the situation changes.

Social psychology is the subfield that studies the behavior of people in groups and the social influences of groups on individuals. Social psychology is an interesting subfield because it invites us to think differently about ourselves and about the causes of behavior. To that extent, it's a valuable topic—anytime we think differently, we expand our intellectual horizons and our critical faculties. I urge you to think about the topics of roles and the importance of situations. I would also like to point out that we are going to examine a number of different topics. I'm going to describe a few famous experiments as we review the topics. Treat these topics separately and try not to combine them in some big picture. The best way to approach social psychology is to keep the topics separate and discrete.

The topics we're going to review are: social roles; attribution; conformity; obedience; helping and altruism; liking; attitudes and cognitive dissonance; and prejudice. That's quite a load of topics, so we had best set sail without hesitation.

A *social role is defined as a set of expectations that govern how we are supposed to act based on age, gender, and occupation.* Some of these expectations are quite explicit—we're told what to think and how to behave. Some of these expectations are implicit and based on observation—we're not told what to think or how to behave, but somehow we do so accordingly.

We expect a professor to act in a certain way. You're surprised when he doesn't. The professor expects students to act in a certain way. He's annoyed when they don't. The salesperson expects the customer to act in a particular way. He drifts to other customers when she doesn't. The customer expects the salesperson to act in a particular way. She takes her business elsewhere when he doesn't.

We expect four-year-old boys to act in a particular way. We expect fourteen-year-old boys to act in a particular way. And we expect forty-four year-old men to act in a particular way—just like the fourteen year olds act. Same thing with girls of various ages.

We assume social roles because that's what we're supposed to do. When we do, we're in the game. We're in the play. We're at the table. *We get respect and maintain our self-respect. And we get information about how to behave.* We know what to do. Everyone is happy and everything runs smoothly.

Think how it was the first day at work. Maybe it's a retail job. Maybe it's a corporate position. You might have been trained, but you're still unsure. You were in the wings, now you're on center stage. What do you do in these situations? You watch what everyone else is doing. You observe. You copy. You imitate. Before you know it, you're one of the gang. In a matter of days, you're an old hand.

When you choose not to play a social role or when you don't know how to act and can't find out how to act—well, you're considered an oddball, a malcontent, a trouble maker. People don't know how to respond to you. And people don't like this. The social wheels go off the tracks and into the ravine. The other actors don't know the lines when a person ad-libs. The audience stares and gasps. This isn't the play they paid to see. If you don't read the role as written, you're not invited back for the matinee.

Assuming social roles sounds like a chore, but it's among the easiest things in the world to accomplish. We do it all the time—just watch the new kid in the playground. We are social creatures. We are built to be social. The first famous experiment I'm going to describe is by Harley, Banks and Zimbardo in 1973. It's called the "Stanford Prison Study" and it was reevaluated by Zimbardo in a book that came out a few years ago called *The Lucifer Effect*.

I'm sure that Harley and Banks are fine men and well known in their circles, but Philip Zimbardo was the lead researcher. You might remember I mentioned his troubles with the bully in the motivation lecture. Zimbardo's a prominent researcher and writer of textbooks and he's been interested in how the principles of social psychology turn ordinary people into destructive and hateful people. This is a theme I'll come back to.

In the prison study Stanford University students were randomly selected to play the roles of prisoners and of prison guards—I once heard James Cagney call prison guards "screws," but that was in a movie. In August, 1971, the basement of the psychology building was converted into a prison. (And, yes, there's an entire building devoted to psychology at Stanford.) The point of the study was to examine how the students would ease into the roles of prisoners and guards. The easement occurred on ice.

The prisoners were picked up by the Palo Alto police, arrested for a bogus robbery, and "booked." Inside the "prison" the prisoners had to wear prison garb. They had to use a bucket for a toilet. They could be strip searched. The guards wore uniforms and black-mirrored sunglasses. Within days a "speedy and terrifying transformation," as Zimbardo described it, occurred in a third of the guards. These guards became dictatorial, cruel, and verbally abusive. The study had to be stopped prematurely after six days of a scheduled fourteen.

The results are impressive and troubling. A number of college students played the role of guard so effectively they became abusive to fellow students. They were liberal, upscale, happening Californians. Probably, they're tan and go surfing after class. They had no experience with prison. Probably, the only prison guards they knew were the screws who tormented James Cagney. But they had the sanction of Stanford University and of the psychology department. They were told they were prison guards and that's what they became.

The students who were selected as prisoners also slipped into the role. The prisoners in one cell rebelled on the second day of the study. One prisoner was placed in solitary confinement—a closet—for going on a hunger strike. Another prisoner started to scream and to curse. He had to be released from the study.

Zimbardo's overall conclusion was that *people easily assume social roles*, even when those roles demand cruelty. The study also demonstrated the influence of obedience, a topic we'll review shortly. Zimbardo instructed the guards to create a sense of fear and powerlessness in the prisoners. He further instructed the guards to take away the prisoners' individualities. They were instructed to act in a domineering way and that's what they did. They had the sanction of the university and of a famous professor and they complied. They were "only following orders."

We have to be careful in generalizing the results, however. The study involved the grand total of twenty four students. Twelve guards. Twelve prisoners. Three of the twelve guards became abusive. This is 25%, but of a total of twelve people. Not exactly the population of California. Not even of Palo Alto. We can look at the results from a different perspective and say that 75% of the guards did not become overly abusive.

The next port on this voyage on the enchanted sea of social psychology is *attribution theory*, which was introduced into psychology by Fritz Heider in the 1950s. I'll define it and describe the fundamental attribution error, the self-serving bias, and the just-world phenomenon. These topics hang together and they hang individually. Remember to treat each topic separately.

We're always interested in explaining our behavior and the behavior of other people. "Why did I do that?" "What makes me do the things I do?" "Why did he do that?" "Why did she do that?"

To what can we attribute the causes of behavior? Social psychologists suggest there are two options. We can attribute the causes of behavior to our *personalities* and to the personalities of the people we interact with. We do the things we do because that's the *kind of people* we are. They do the things they do because that's the *kind of people* they are. Or we can attribute the causes of behavior to the *situations* we're in. We do the kinds of things that we do, not because of who we are or of some intrinsic element of our personalities, but because of the situations we happen to be in. They do the kinds of things that they do, not because of some intrinsic element of their personalities, but because of the situations they happen to be in.

Consider this example. You're behind me on line as I go through customs in the train station. An economically-challenged person—we use to call them "beggars" in the former days of blunt speech—walks up and asks if I can help him out with some loose change. "Hey, Mack, can you spare a dime?" he asks. He calls me "Mack" because he doesn't know my name. I reach in my pocket and give him a whole dollar. You see this and are impressed, as well you should be. You attribute my generosity to my personality. You think that I'm a really nice man. If you see this happen after you heard this lecture, you might attribute my generosity to something in the situation rather than to my personality. "He must have got paid," you think. "He must have won a lottery." "He must know that people are watching and he wants everyone to think well of him." "He's trying to impress the lady on line ahead of him."

Consider this example. A student gets a high grade on the psychology quiz. He looks at the grade and thinks, "This proves it—I really am a smart person." I look at him gloating and think something in the situation is responsible for the high grade. "If he got a high grade, the quiz was too easy." "I better make the next one more difficult." "I better move the desks further apart."

We attribute the causes of behavior to either persons or to situations. A more sophisticated analysis might examine the *interaction of persons and situations*, but generally we tend to attribute behavior either to personalities or to situations. The *fundamental attribution error is to overestimate the importance of personality and to underestimate the importance of the situatio*n. Even as I speak, the fundamental attribution error is being made all along the Upper East Side of Manhattan. The error is being made in other places, too.

Social psychology comes down on the side of the situation. Many people prefer to focus on personality because they feel in control of their lives and thoughts. If I am in control of myself, so must the people in train stations and in classrooms be in control of themselves. There's an entire subfield of psychology that makes the fundamental attribution error in the eyes of social psychologists. This is the subfield of personality psychology. Religion and the legal system prefer to focus on personality rather than on situations. We feel we are personally and morally responsible regardless of the situation we're in. If I commit a sin, religion says I can't blame someone else. "Choose this day whom you will serve," the *Book of Joshua* (24:15) insists. Similarly, if I commit a crime, the law says I can't blame my upbringing or my neighborhood. Social psychology takes a different slant. Good people can do bad things in particular situations. I suppose the opposite is true—bad people can do good things in particular situations.

Consider the fundamental attribution error in the context of my examples. You see me give the economically-challenged man a dollar and you think that, deep down, I'm a really nice man. But maybe I did just get paid. Maybe I did win a lottery. Maybe I want to impress people. Maybe I want to impress the lady standing ahead of me on line.

A student got a high grade on the quiz. He thinks he's a smart person. I know differently. The quiz was too easy. The next one needs to be more difficult. And the desks were a little close. If we neglect to consider the situation, we overlook chunks of possibilities when it comes to the causes of behavior.

The self-serving bias follows from the fundamental attribution error. The *self-serving bias suggests that we tend to credit our successes and our reputable traits to our personalities and to credit our failures and our disreputable traits to the situations we're in.* We tend to want to see ourselves in a favorable light. The self-serving bias is also happening all along the Upper East Side.

Consider my examples. You see me hand the economically-challenged man a dollar and you say, "Sir, you are a nice person." I blush at the compliment and publicly dismiss the idea, but I think, "I really am a nice person." I don't respond, "I'm really a miserable miser. You must have caught me on a day I took off from being cheap." I give the quizzes back and tell the student, "Good work." The student blushes at the compliment and shrugs in agreement. The student doesn't say, "This quiz was so easy even I scored high."

Let's reverse the examples. You overhear me telling the economically-challenged man to get out of my face. You say, "That wasn't very nice. You're a mean person." If I don't tell you to mind your own business, I probably don't agree. I don't say, "Yes, I can't help it. I am a mean person." Instead I come up with a reason—an attribution—that blames the situation. "I'm late for work." "I got a demotion at work." "I lost my wallet." "I'm worried about losing my job." I give the quizzes back and this time the student scored low. "I know you'll do better on the next quiz," I say. The student doesn't respond, "I'm an intellectually-challenged person who doesn't belong in college." Instead the student thinks something along the lines that the quiz was too difficult or too tricky.

Notice that in these examples we took the credit when credit was due and we blamed the situation when something unflattering and blameworthy occurred.

Another variant of the fundamental attribution error is the just-world phenomenon. This concept was introduced into psychology by

Melvin Lerner in the 1960s. *When we exhibit the just-world phenomenon we believe that people get what they deserve on account of their personalities.* And we believe that people *deserve what they get.* As you might guess, people all along the Upper East Side are demonstrating the just-world phenomenon.

I suppose we commit the just-world phenomenon because we have a need to believe the world is a fair and just place. We want to believe the world is an orderly place, a place where events are organized in a causal manner, and a place where events do not happen by chance. We want to believe that the world is a place where fair is fair, where right is right, and where people get what they deserve. The just-world phenomenon may be psychologically real in the sense that people demonstrate it cognitively, but it is not empirically real in the sense that it does not correspond to the way the world works.

The just-world phenomenon can be noted in the largest political and religious arenas. We believe that rich people are rich because, deep down, they are talented, intelligent and competent people. We are so enamored of rich people that we glamorize them. We will even vote for them for mayor, governor and president. In my country of New Jersey we elected Jon Corzine, a former Wall St. executive and millionaire, governor. People voted for him because they assumed he was talented, intelligent and competent. Otherwise he wouldn't be rich. He turned out to be a catastrophic failure as governor. Decades ago there was a colorful billionaire named Ross Perot who ran for president on a third party ticket in 1992. He didn't win the presidency, but if memory serves correctly—often it doesn't—we owe Bill Clinton's victory to him. (He siphoned votes from the Republican candidate, the first George Bush.) People voted for Perot because they assumed he was talented, intelligent and competent. Otherwise he wouldn't be rich. Perot turned out to be an oddball who believed people were following and spying on him and, who knows?, maybe he was right.

We believe the reverse, too. Poor people are poor because they are untalented, intellectually challenged and incompetent. After all, people get what they deserve. If we're poor it must be because we're not up to speed in the game of life.

The belief that the rich are competent and the poor are incompetent is so pervasive in our culture it has become part of certain religions. There are sects that believe that being rich is a sign of God's grace. If you are rich, this is proof you are one of "The Elect." If you are poor, this is a sign that you are out of favor with God. I once heard a religious radio broadcast from the country of New York. The preacher called poverty a "sin." Poor people are sinners. The only way to absolve oneself of this particular sin was to send the preacher a donation.

When we step back from the fundamental attribution error and consider the situation in our analysis, we see that there are many reasons why people are rich. Yes, there are talented, intelligent and competent people among the rich. There are also rich people who inherited their wealth. There are rich people who got their wealth through criminal activities. And there are rich people who got their wealth through incredible luck—they are at "The right place at the right time," which is situational, if nothing else. There are poor people who are untalented, intellectually challenged and incompetent. There are also poor people who lost their wealth or made bad choices or faced bad situations or who never got a break. There are just as many situational reasons for poverty as there are for wealth.

Consider the just-world phenomenon in another context. A tragedy happens and we think the victim "Got what he or she deserved." So he stayed out late and walked home through the park. He should have known what happens to people who walk through parks at night. So she was sexually molested. She shouldn't have been wearing provocative clothes. She shouldn't have entered the bar alone. She shouldn't have been alone in the park.

Years ago, a murder was committed during the act of sex in Central Park. I don't know if this kind of thing commonly goes on in Central Park—sex, that is, not murder. A hulking sociopath strangled a petite young woman. He claimed that sex got rough and he strangled her in a defensive act. During the trial his lawyers brought in the victim's sexual history and claimed she was sexually insatiable. It got so bad, the state of New York changed the trial laws involving sex crimes. We have this murderer to thank for the fact that a victim's sexual history cannot be introduced at trial. The point his lawyers were making was that she had only herself to blame. If she wasn't so sexually insatiable, she'd be alive.

Fred Thompson, Watergate lawyer, actor, and failed presidential candidate, exhibited the just-world phenomenon in a blog about the massacre at Virginia Tech in 2007. Thompson wrote that the massacre wouldn't have happened—or wouldn't have been so bloody—if students and faculty could bring guns into classrooms. We see the reason Fred Thompson didn't win the Republican nomination for president—he's an ass. I understand I'm making the fundamental attribution error calling Fred Thompson an ass, but I believe I'm correct in his case. Incidentally, the fact that Fred Thompson didn't win the Republican nomination is proof that God exists.

Consider the situation. A maniac enters a class and starts shooting. A student—a hero student, I should say—ducks behind a desk, reaches in his book bag, pulls out a handgun, and shoots the maniac between the eyes. I think I saw this happen in a movie one time. If this student doesn't do this—if he stays in his seat and dies—he has only himself to blame.

The just-world phenomenon can also be observed in our romantic relationships. Think what happens when we break up. We blame the other person for the break up and for the emotional pain. We say, "You got what you deserved. It's your fault you got hurt because you loved me." The folk singer Gordon Lightfoot has a lyric about the same unhappy end of a once true love. "That's what you get for loving me." I'd sing it, but you'd lose respect for me. Besides, I don't know any other lyrics.

The just-world phenomenon may be true in a psychological sense, but it's not true in an objective sense. I'll prove the just-world phenomenon is not objectively true. If it were true, I'd be on a yacht in the Mediterranean Sea and Kate Winslet would be serving me fried chicken.

Let's move onto the next port. This is conformity. Conformity means exactly what you believe it means—*conformity is adjusting one's behavior and opinions to those of a group.*

Sometimes conformity is done consciously and explicitly. We stand in front of a mirror and primp until we get the look just right. Sometimes conformity is done unconsciously and implicitly. We go along and adjust our behavior and opinions without thinking about it. Consider what happens when a person yawns. Everyone in the vicinity yawns. And consider what happens in long-term relationships. We start to use the same phrases and intonations as our partners. And we may start to mimic their nonverbal behavior.

I experienced a pristine example of conformity on the subway recently. A group of fourteen and fifteen year olds boarded the PATH train at Exchange Place. I instantly perked up and held my valise tighter. They looked like trouble. But then I remembered social psychology and conformity. I started watching them from the corner of my eye. They wore the same dark clothing. They wore the same baseball caps. They wore the same red jackets. They wore the same baggy trousers. They wore the same colored boxer shorts. They used the same hand gestures. They used the same swearwords. They laughed at the same places. They spoke at the same volume. I'm sure each of them believed he was unique. But they were peas ripened in the same adolescent pod. They could have been grown on the same tree or planted in the same pubescent patch.

We conform for the same purposes we play social roles—*to get information and to maintain our self-respect*. If we know what to do, we feel we belong in a group. If we don't know what to do, we withdraw. We want to know what to do and we want to belong. We want to be included in group activities. We want a "place at the table," as the expression goes. None of us want to be ostracized. *Ostracism* is an ugly word for an ugly concept. Ostracism means to be left out and not to be included in group activities. Ostracism means to be shunned.

What would happen in the gang of teens if one of them wore preppie clothes or a blue jacket? What would happen if one of them wore briefs instead of boxer shorts? I tend to think this teen would not be riding in the same car. And think of this example. Think what would happen if you went out to eat with a group of co-workers or classmates. Everyone at the table expresses the same opinion. It is not your opinion. They like a particular movie. You hated it. They like a particular politician. You hate the guy. What do you do when it comes your turn to speak? Maybe you say nothing. Maybe you choose your words carefully. Maybe you pretend to go along with the group. Maybe you say what you think and tell the truth. That's a risky thing to do because you may not be invited back. The group doesn't want a dissident. The group doesn't want to hear that it's wrong. The group wants unanimity.

So I'm sitting with someone. I say, "I loved the movie *Titanic*." The other person says, "That movie stunk." This statement implies that I'm wrong and that I don't know what I'm talking about when it comes to movies. I get offended and I may not want to talk to this person again. I certainly don't want to talk about movies. Consider the opposite. I say, "I loved the movie *Titanic*." The other person agrees, "I loved *Titanic*, too." Well, this person has agreed with me. The person says our opinions are correct. The person inflated my self-respect and told me in other words that great minds think alike. I'm so happy I may go the movies with the person.

As I say, there are a number of famous experiments in social psychology. One involves conformity. It was performed by Solomon Asch at Yale University in the 1950s. A student enters the lab. Other students are seated at a table. Asch says the purpose of the experiment is to study group decision making. What this student doesn't know is that he's a "dupe." A dupe is a person who doesn't know what's going on. I frequently play the role of a dupe. In fact, I frequently play the role of a super dupe. What the student doesn't know is that the experiment involves conformity and that everyone at the table is part of the act.

The group is shown a series of cards on which there are three black lines. The group has to compare a test line with one of the three black lines and come to a decision which of the three matches the test line. A few cards are shown. They go around the table and everyone agrees. The answers are correct. Everything matches. The dupe settles in and thinks, "This is easy." But then the key card appears. The first person makes an outrageous mistake. The line he's chosen clearly does not match the test line. It differs by a few inches. The dupe perks up. "What?" his expression begs. The second person agrees with the decision. So does the third. So does the fourth. The lines clearly don't match. Now it's the dupe's turn. What is he going to say? Is he going to agree with the obviously wrong decision? Is he going to disagree?

I understand you're all blunt-speaking New Yorkers, but Asch discovered something different and something troubling. Asch discovered that about one third of the sample "went along" with the wrong decision. That's one third. Thirty three percent. The numbers add up quickly. Three people out of ten. Thirty three people out of a hundred. Three hundred thirty three people out of a thousand. You can do the arithmetic as well as I. A sizeable percentage of intelligent college students went along with the group's decision when it was obviously incorrect. We hate to think what the percentages are in the lumpen class.

Asch debriefed the dupes who went along. "Did you know it was the incorrect decision?" Every dupe did. Asch asked, "Why did you go along if you knew it was the incorrect decision?" The majority of the dupes replied that they did not want to rock the boat and ruin the rapport of the group. That's how strong the pressure is to conform.

I'm reminded of a scene in Monty Python's movie *The Meaning of Life*. The Angel of Death comes to a high-brow dinner party. The guests are escorted one by one to "the other place." One of the guests asks Death what did them in. "It was the salmon," Death answers. The last guest follows the procession through the Pearly Gates. "But I had pot roast," he says.

Asch discovered that conformity increases under the following conditions. The group size is small. The group decision is unanimous. We admire the group. We are anxious and insecure. We have no prior commitment to the topic. And we are being watched while in the group.

There may be hope—a glimmer—if we reverse these conditions. The group size is large. Dissenters express their opinions—if someone disagrees ahead of us we feel we have an ally and are emboldened to dissent. We don't particularly admire the group. We have a commitment to the topic—we'd all turn into stalwart New Yorkers if it were a topic we cared about rather than the trivial topic of estimating the length of lines. Finally, we will dissent if we can do so privately rather than publicly.

Group decisions are more extreme than individual decisions. One reason for the extremity is the anonymity of being in a group. If we make a decision by our lonesome, the burden falls entirely on us. But we can hide in groups and the responsibility can be spread among all the members. Another reason for making extreme decisions is the pressure to achieve unanimity. This tendency is called *groupthink*. It was first described by Irwin Janis in 1972. Group members do not want to criticize one another—or to criticize the leadership of the group. Remember Asch's experiment—dupes did not want to ruin the rapport of a group they just joined and had no special attachment to. The pressure not to criticize the group or its leadership intensifies if we are long-term members of the group or if we value the group highly.

Groups that exhibit groupthink demonstrate the following characteristics. Members do not criticize the decisions the group makes. Members do not examine evidence that contradicts their beliefs. Members do not examine alternatives. Members are selective in the evidence they collect to support their beliefs. Members demonstrate the *confirmation bias*, which is the tendency to establish lenient standards for evidence that supports a group's position and strict standards for evidence that contradicts the position. Members pressure one another to conform and cooperate. Finally, dissenters are not invited back.

What happens is the group becomes more extreme. There is no dissenting voice. There is no competing view. There is no intellectual brake on a runaway train of ideas. Without dissenting views, the group becomes more convinced that its decisions are correct. The group becomes convinced that it is invulnerable.

I saw groupthink in action in my heyday as a Kennedy assassination researcher. The buffs were a closed society that would never entertain the possibility that Lee Harvey Oswald shot President Kennedy. They would entertain any possibility that he did not murder the president, which led to extraordinary theories that promptly lost contact with reality. The buffs dismissed the value of criticism and refutation. Anyone who disagreed with their view was ostracized and viewed as an undercover agent or a dope, which I suppose is worse than being a dupe. If a person disagreed with them, the person was shown the door in the lobby of the hotel and not invited back to the following year's convention.

I'm not going to downplay the importance of the conspiracy crowd. They became quite influential in America in the early 1990s. Probably, a majority of Americans agreed with them. Groupthink is observed in more important political contexts than in the mysterious land of conspiracy. Janis studied it in the context of the April, 1961, Bay of Pigs debacle and in the October, 1962, Cuban Missile crises, which was the closest the world ever came to a nuclear exchange between the United States and the Soviet Union. In the Bay of Pigs crises dissenters in the Kennedy administration did not openly express opposition to the invasion of Cuba. They were encouraged by the more aggressive presidential advisors not to disagree. In the Cuban Missile crises debate and dissent were encouraged. To our good fortune, President Kennedy kept his cool and actively sought out contrary views to the dominant military option of blowing up the world. President Kennedy learned from the errors in decision making in the Bay of Pigs disaster. He once said to the effect that it takes more courage to stand up to one's associates than to one's enemies.

Let's move onto the next topic—*obedience*. In conformity people adjust their behaviors and opinions to those of a group. A group informs a person what to do and think. *In obedience people adjust their behaviors and opinions to those of a leader.* A leader tells a person what to do and think. The leader may be a parent, a teacher, a cleric, a manager, a military officer, or a *fuhrer*.

Perhaps the most famous experiments in psychology involve obedience. These were the experiments performed by Stanley Milgram at Yale University. The experiment was so famous it was made into a movie called *The Tenth Level* staring William Shatner as Stanley Milgram. (This was in Shatner's lean years between the *Star Trek* television series and the *Star Trek* movies.) Milgram was born in New York City in 1933. He attended Queens College and earned a doctorate from Harvard University. He taught at Harvard for a few years and then spent the rest of his career at CUNY in your country of New York. He died prematurely in 1984.

Let's look at the original experiment in detail. All told, Milgram conducted twenty four experimental variations involving more than seven hundred participants. In the first experiment Milgram recruited forty male volunteers by newspaper and mail solicitation. All volunteers were between twenty and fifty years of age. The experimenter was a thirty-one-year-old male teacher. He was not Milgram. It frequently happens in research that the originator of an experiment does not actually perform it.

The volunteers were dupes, which as you know is a role in which the person does not know the true purpose of the experiment. They were told the purpose of the experiment was to study the effect of punishment on learning. The true purpose of the experiment was to study obedience. If not obedience, then compliance with leadership and with instructions.

Each dupe met the experimenter and the second person involved in the experiment—this was a forty-seven-year-old male. Slips were drawn to see who would play the roles of "teacher" and "student." The procedure was rigged so that the dupe was always the teacher. The person who played the role of the student was part of the experiment. The teacher didn't know that.

The student was strapped into something that looked like an electric chair. In front of the chair were four switches that indicated the student's responses. The experimenter told the teacher and the student that the punishment involved electric shock. They were further told that the shocks would be painful but would cause no permanent tissue damage. A test was conducted at low voltage. The student flinched. The machine worked.

The teacher and experimenter go into a second room. The teacher sits in front of a console with thirty marked switches ranging from fifteen volts to four hundred fifty volts in increments of fifteen volts. The last switch is marked in red and reads "Danger, severe shock." Atop the console are four light bulbs. They signal the student's answers.

The student is to master what is called *paired-associate learning*. This is a common technique in verbal learning in which a person has to memorize the responses to a list of stimulus words. For example, whenever the teacher said "blue" the student has to answer "cloud." Whenever the student said "fence" the student has to answer "cow." Whenever the teacher said "chair" the student has to answer "toast." The student indicates his answer from a list of four choices by pressing a switch that lights up one of the four bulbs on the teacher's console. Of course, the student always chooses the wrong answer.

The teacher is to shock the student for every wrong answer and to go up one level after every mistake. The dependent variable in the study was the level of shock the teachers stopped at. There never was any shock—the teacher doesn't know this.

The results of the experiment were unexpected and shocking. Five teachers stopped at three hundred volts—this is twenty levels of shock into the procedure. Four teachers stopped at three hundred fifteen volts. Two teachers stopped at three hundred thirty volts. One stopped at three hundred forty five volts, one at three hundred sixty volts, and one at three hundred seventy five volts. Twenty six of the sample of forty proceeded to four hundred fifty volts, the maximum level of shock. This is 65% or two thirds of the sample.

The student stopped responding after three hundred volts. No bulb blinked on when the teacher asked the questions. The teacher was told to treat silence as a wrong answer. For ten questions there is no response. The teacher talks to himself and shocks an invisible and silent student. When you think about it, this is a really strange situation.

The published report of the experiment indicated that as the session progressed some of the teachers "… were observed to sweat, tremble, stutter, bite their lips, groan and dig their fingernails into their flesh." Fourteen teachers engaged in "nervous laughter and smiling." Three teachers showed "seizures," one so violently the experiment had to be stopped. It's not clear what Milgram meant by "seizures."

Clearly, the teachers were upset by what they were doing. But they kept doing it. The experimenter did not engage in intimidation if a teacher hesitated to continue. The experimenter used four "prods" to get the teachers to continue. These prods were simple statements. "Please continue." "The experiment requires that you continue." "It is absolutely essential that you continue." "You have no choice, you must go on."

There are a few factors that may have contributed to the obedient behavior of the teachers. The experiment took place in a prestigious university. The experiment would not have been condoned by the university administration if it were unsafe. The student was a volunteer and his role was assigned by what appeared to be chance. The student did nothing to stop the experiment. Presumably, he could have hollered for the shocks to stop. The experimenter assured everyone that the shocks resulted in no permanent damage. The experiment lasted only a few minutes.

The results of the experiment amazed people. No one predicted the percentage of participants who would proceed to the highest level. Milgram was severely criticized for using deception and for the upsetment he placed on the teachers. Milgram defended himself against the charge of deception by replying that deception was the only way he could have attained valid results. If the teachers knew the shocks were fake, the experiment would have served no purpose. In fact, deception was quite common in experiments at the time period—this was the early 1960s. That is no longer the case. Today, experimenters have to obtain "informed consent" from the participants in a research study. Experimenters have to let the participants know the purpose of the study and the procedure ahead of time. This change was due in part to the uproar over Milgram's research.

The criticism that Milgram failed to adequately debrief and counsel the teachers is less easy to deny. The teacher met the student after the experiment and saw that he was unharmed. The experimenter briefly explained the purpose of the experiment and thanked the teacher. That was about the extent of the debriefing. The teachers were never told the shocks were not real—they left the building believing they had shocked a person. Milgram sent the teachers a letter explaining the procedure and the purpose of the experiment a few months after the research ended and a psychiatrist was made available by Yale if anyone wanted to talk about the experience. Few participants availed themselves of the opportunity.

Milgram seriously underestimated the deeply troubling and long lasting effects the experiment had on the teachers. A psychologist named Gina Perry tracked down some of the surviving teachers. She found that the teachers were ashamed and disturbed by what they did. They realized what they were capable of and they didn't like what they discovered about themselves. They felt angry and betrayed when they learned *they were the targets of the research* and not the student. This anger and sense of betrayal stayed with them for years.

We think of the 65% who proceeded to four hundred fifty volts as Nazis in the making and as sadistic and unconcerned with the violence they perpetrated on a helpless person. (Milgram may not have thought of the teachers in these terms, but the Nazi atrocities in the Second World War gave impetus to his research.) Perry found quite the opposite. The teachers were moral individuals who were horrified by what they did.

Regardless of his cavalier attitude toward the participants, the result of Milgram's experiment is troubling—"Ordinary people … without any particular hostility … can become agents in a terribly destructive process." We have to assume the twenty six teachers who proceeded to the maximum voltage were ordinary people without any psychopathology. Yet with the slimmest of provocation, they were willing to shock a stranger who had done them no harm.

Social psychology stresses the situation more than personality. The situation these people were in caused them to act the way they did. The role they were playing as teachers resulted in their grim progression to four hundred fifty volts. Perhaps a more sophisticated analysis would report that something in their personalities responded to the situation. We like to think we'd act differently. We like to think we wouldn't shock a stranger or that we would quit at a low level of shock, but we can't say with certainty until we step into the role that situation provides.

The social psychological principles of conformity and obedience are directly relevant to crimes and to historical cruelties. After the Second World War some of the Nazi leaders were brought to justice in Nuremburg. Their defense reeks of these principles. They claimed they were good soldiers, a band of Nazi brothers. They claimed they were "only following orders." Hitler told them what to do. They said Hitler was *Der Fuhrer*. He should be the one on trial. I think if Hitler were on trial he would claim that he was "only following orders"—his own orders.

The Nazi leaders avoided the fundamental attribution error—I'm not sure this is to their credit. They claimed they were not bad men. It was the war that made them do the horrible things that they did. "Don't blame us," they insinuated. "Sure, bad things happened, but once you unleash the dogs of war, what do you expect?"

Jump forward in time to the Vietnam War. There were atrocities in the Vietnam War, as there are in all wars. A notorious one occurred at a place called My Lai in March, 1968. Five hundred civilians were killed there by American troops. A lieutenant named William Calley was court-martialed and sentenced to a few years in prison. Calley's defense was much the same as the defense the Nazis offered at Nuremberg. "I was among my band of brothers." "I was only following orders." "When you unleash the dogs of war, bad things happen."

Jump forward in time to the Second Iraq War and to the Abu Ghrail prison debacle. Even the people who live in Benson Hurst can predict the defense the prison guards made.

Personality psychologists stress the personalities of the culprits. So does the legal system. So does the media and popular culture. The Nazi leaders, Lt. Calley, the Abu Ghrail guards—they were bad people. They were bad apples. Social psychologists would not necessarily disagree. But social psychologists would also insist that we examine the situation. As much as there are bad apples, there are bad barrels. There may be elements in situations that cause decent and ordinary people to act in ways they would not ordinarily act in and do evil and vicious things. As the saying goes—if we take decent and ordinary people and place them in hell, hellish things are going to happen.

Decent and ordinary people can do indecent and extraordinary things in particular situations. We don't need spectacular explanations or out-of-the-ordinary concepts to explain such behavior. We need only consider concepts like conformity and obedience. And we have to remember that people behave differently in groups than when they are alone.

There are, of course, people who are born bad. They're rotten apples from the womb. And there are people who are exposed to such horrible upbringings that they lose their connection to humanity. And there are many other people who do aggressive and violent deeds without a history of psychopathology or trauma. Right away, we start thinking inside the box of personality. Right away, we make the fundamental attribution error. There are social psychological principles that may help explain why good apples turn bad. An authority figure tells us what to do. It may be *Der Fuhrer*. It may be Lt. Calley's superior officer. We conform to what everyone is doing. Everyone in my Berlin neighborhood hates the Jews. Everyone in my band of brothers is shooting at the villagers. There is comfort in conforming. There may even be prestige. It is difficult to disobey and to act in a contrarian manner, especially in war, which is an exceptional situation.

There may be reinforcement for going along and acting in an aggressive manner. No one wants to be just a soldier. We want to move up the ranks. We don't do that if we act in a contrarian manner. Consider that there have been brutal organizations like the "SS" and "elite guards" that were treated in a deferential manner for performing the most violent acts.

Learning psychologists talk about the concept of *habituation*—we get use to repeating acts. Social psychologists talk about the *mere exposure effect*—we grow accustomed to things we see frequently. We're horrified the first time we see violence. We're afraid the first time we see bloodshed. As the violence continues, we're no longer horrified. As the bloodshed continues, we're no longer afraid.

We can blame the victim, as in the just-world phenomenon. We can provide self-serving justifications for the evil that's done. The Nazis justified killing Jewish children on the grounds that the children would seek revenge when they grew up.

We can use euphemisms and double talk for what we do. "I'm not killing civilians, I'm engaging in collateral damage." "I'm not bombing civilian targets, I'm bombing soft targets." "I'm not hurting you, I'm chastising you and it's for your own good." "I'm not torturing you, I'm engaged in an enhanced interrogation technique."

Philip Zimbardo and others suggest that there are two crucial factors involved in turning good people into bad people. The first factor is *reduced accountability* for acting in an evil manner. If people believe they can get away with committing an evil deed or if they are told a leader takes responsibility, then they may act in a way they would not ordinarily demonstrate.

The second factor is reduced responsibility through *anonymity*. I am not seen—I can get away with an evil deed. I can vanish in a mass of soldiers or rioters. I can wear a disguise. Notice how people in violent organizations like the Ku Klux Klan covered their faces so no one could see who they were. Soldiers rub war paint on. Executioners wear hoods—today they stand in separate rooms from the criminal. The criminal also wears a hood—I can turn the electricity on without hesitation because I don't see his face. The face provides an identity and it's hidden from me.

I sometimes think anonymity plays a role in the carnage on our highways. Once they get in their cars otherwise law-abiding individuals turn into homicidal maniacs who break every rule and defy every standard of safety. I wouldn't think of hitting you with a baseball bat. But I wouldn't think twice about running you off the road and into the woods if you're driving too slow ahead of me. In the first case with the bat—I see you and you see me. There is accountability. There is no anonymity. There is anonymity behind the steering wheel—I can't see you and you can't see me, so I can drive aggressively. And there is little or no accountability—it is rare that a driver gets pulled over for driving aggressively.

Let's move onto the next social psychological topic. This is *liking*. We say we like a person and we promptly make the fundamental attribution error. We like you because, gosh darn it, you're likeable. Deep down and at the superficies, too, you're a likeable person.

Social psychologists say that may be true. There are gems among people like there are diamonds in the coal yard. Social psychologists suggest that we should examine situational factors in liking another person. We tend to like people who provide reinforcements and who take away our punishments. We tend to like people to whom we provide reinforcements and remove punishments. The first statement is intuitively obvious. The second statement can be explained in part by the concept of cognitive dissonance, which I'll describe in a few minutes unless something bad happens.

Social psychologists suggest we like people who live near us and who we encounter frequently. This is called the *proximity effect*. It is difficult to live near or with people we actively dislike or despise. And it is difficult to carry on a relationship with people at a distance. Maybe we can stay in a relationship with another person over the Internet or over the phone. What is lacking, of course, is the physical part of the relationship—what is lacking is touch and the subtleties of facial communication. He lives in North Bronx, she lives in Coney Island. Professor Ford can fly to Orlando from the Atlantic City airport in less time than it takes him to travel from the Grand Concourse to Surf Avenue.

The proximity effect is similar to the mere exposure effect I mentioned previously. The two may even be the same. We tend to get attached to and to like things we encounter a lot. I recall the cranky driver on the BX 55 bus back when I was taking courses. In the year I rode on his bus I never said more to him than "Hello." He never even said that. All he did was grunt after I paid the fare. Then one day he was gone and replaced by a different driver. I felt bad. I missed him. I hoped nothing bad happened to him.

The mere exposure effect may underlie advertising. Think of all the Macy's commercials we've seen and of all the Old Navy commercials. They're awful, but they don't have to be good. It may even be better if they're obnoxious and in bad taste. To be effective, they just have to be repeated and repeated and repeated. The next time we need a bottle of cologne—what store name pops into our head? The next time we need to buy our kids clothing—what store name pops into our head? Advertisers wouldn't spend millions if these tasteless and tacky commercials weren't effective in emptying our wallets.

Social psychologists stress that we like people who look like us, act like us, and express the same opinions. This is called the *similarity effect*. Think, for example, of picking a hitchhiker up—I don't know if people still hitchhike. If they do, I'm not about to pick up someone who looks like a Goth. I am more likely to pick up someone who looks, I don't know, like me. And a Goth isn't going to pick up someone who looks like me, unless he's going to rough me up in the back seat and steal my paycheck.

The reasons why the similarity effect is so important in liking aren't hard to find. There's a certain comfort factor in being with our own kind—in being with people of the same faith and occupation and educational level. We can talk about things easily. We don't have to explain everything. A lot of things in conversations are understood as background or as context.

The similarity effect may be seen in the physical appearance of couples. I've noticed that attractive people date and marry and that appearance-challenged people date and marry. In the old rough days we use to call appearance-challenged people—we can't use the term "ugly" any longer. Let's just say these people leave a lot to be desired in the looks department.

According to social psychologists "Birds of a feather flock together." Like attracts like. Like stays with like. Opposites may attract initially, but opposites don't necessarily stay together. The main reason significant others turn into insignificant others is *dissimilarity*. Two people have nothing in common. He likes professional wrestling. She likes the ballet. He likes beer. She likes champagne. He likes television dinners. She likes gourmet meals. He likes to sit in the parlor all night. She likes to travel. He has a high school education. She has a doctorate in experimental psychology. There's nothing to talk about. There's nothing to say. It takes too much effort to communicate. He goes one way. She goes another way. Breaking up isn't hard to do.

The next topic I'll like to cover is *altruism* or *helping behavior*. Many people make the fundamental attribution error when they see one person help another. Think of my example of giving the beggar—excuse me, economically-challenged person—a dollar in the train station. You think, "What a nice man you are." You may even say it.

Maybe I am a nice man. Maybe something else is responsible for my parting with a dollar. As you know, social psychologists stress situational variables. There may be an element in the situation that induces me to help another person. A more sophisticated analysis may focus on the interaction between personality and situational factors.

One variable stressed by social psychologists when it comes to altruism is *similarity*. We tend to help other people who look like us, act like us, and say the things we say. There may be a self-respect issue here. There may be a safety issue—I don't know your kind, so I better not risk helping you. There may be an informational issue here. If you resemble me, I may be aware that you need help. If you don't resemble me, I may not be aware that you need help. We see this on train platforms, where one drug addict helps another, or where a member of

Alcoholics Anonymous helps an intoxicated person, or where one senior citizen helps another. I don't use drugs—I don't know when a person is in danger. I'm a teetotaler—I don't know when an intoxicated person is in danger. I'm middle-aged—I don't know when an elderly person is experiencing difficulty.

Of course, when it comes to providing help, there is a *competency* issue. Can I provide the kind of help that's needed? If I don't know first aid, I may do more harm than good if I try to help. If I don't know how intoxicated people act, it may do me more harm than good.

Another variable stressed by social psychologists when it comes to helping is *normative social influence.* Do we believe it is proper to help another person? Do we believe it is our responsibility to help? Consider the economically-challenged person in the train station. Do we see him as responsible for both the problems he faces and for the solutions? Do we see him as responsible for the problem and not for the solution? Or do we see the reverse? He's not responsible for falling into poverty, but he is responsible for getting himself back on his feet and into legitimate employment than standing in train stations and hassling kind-hearted commuters. Finally, do we see him as responsible for neither the problems or for the solutions to his difficulties?

Helping a person provides rewards. We feel good about helping. It is a Spiritual and Corporal Act of Mercy to help. It earns us points in the cosmic arcade. It may even earn us merits in this life. Helping proves how good we are. Not helping a person is rarely punished—it's rarely noticed. There are always ways to justify not helping. Only a handful of states have laws in which not helping can get us fined. In Wisconsin we can get fined as much as five hundred dollars for not helping. I don't know what the fine for not helping in Vermont is, but this being the state of Vermont, the fine must be steep.

Another variable stressed by social psychologists is *mood* or *emotional state.* If we are in a *happy mood*, we are more likely to help another person. Happy people are helpful people. Angry or frightened people are not helpful. Consider what would follow if a student scored a hundred on the quiz and noticed another student picking up papers off the floor in the corridor. This student is in a happy mood. The chances are good he'll bend and help pick the papers up. Consider what would follow if a student scored fifty on the quiz and noticed another student picking up papers off the corridor floor. This student is not in a happy mood, unless fifty was an improvement over what he scored on an earlier quiz. He's not going to be in the mood to help pick up notes. We're lucky he doesn't walk over the scattered papers.

The relationship between happiness and helpfulness can be useful to parents. If parents want their children to help clean up their rooms or do household chores, they should get the children in happy moods. There are lots of ways to do this—fun and games, jokes, tickling, horsing around, cartoons on the television, a crayon gripped in the front teeth.

The most notorious variable with respect to altruism is the *number of people present who can offer help*. In the early morning hours of Friday, March 13, 1962, Kitty Genovese was stabbed to death outside her home in Kew Gardens, Queens. She was a young barmaid on her way home from work. She was attacked and left for dead. The murderer, a thug named Winston Moseley, subsequently returned to the scene and killed her. The murder was particularly heinous and made international headlines since newspaper articles—and, later, a book—claimed that thirty eight witnesses heard Kitty cry for help. None of the thirty eight called the police or came to her assistance.

The initial concept why no one acted was called *bystander apathy*. This concept seemed to validate everything negative about the cold cruel city. People—Kitty's neighbors—stood by and did nothing. They hid in their apartments. They plugged their fingers in their ears so as not to hear the screams. They turned their backs and let a defenseless young woman get murdered.

Later analyses suggested a different interpretation. The concept is called *diffusion of responsibility*. No one acted because the responsibility to act spread among the members of the group. Responsibility was not focalized. It was diffuse. The guy on the fourth floor expected the guy on the second floor to act. The guy on the second floor expected the guy on the fourth floor to act. No one acted because everyone expected someone else to act. In fact, this may have happened in Kitty's murder. A neighbor named Sam Koshkin saw the first attack from a sixth floor window. He wanted to call the police, but his wife stopped him and advised, "There must be thirty calls by now."

Paradoxically, *a person's chance of getting help improves the fewer people are present to offer help*. The more people present, the greater the diffusion of responsibility. The more people present, the less each person feels responsible for acting—or for not acting. The fewer people present, the less diffusion of responsibility occurs. The fewer people present, the less each person can avoid the responsibility for acting—or for not acting. So we're in a restaurant with fifty people and someone starts to choke. Everyone hesitates. Everyone looks at everyone else. Who's going to help? Who's going to perform the Heimlich maneuver? In this situation a lot of people can shirk the responsibility. Change the example. We're in a restaurant with one other person and he starts to choke. Well, we can be a thorough lout and slip out the back door or we can try to perform the Heimlich maneuver. In this situation we can't shirk the responsibility. There's only one pair of shoulders for responsibility to land on—ours.

In this class there's an opportunity to learn a lot of useful information. Here's a particularly useful piece of advice that may save your life. If you're walking, say in the bus station, and you feel faint, or if you're walking with someone who faints, don't yell, "Help!" or "Somebody, help!" These open-ended statements guarantee diffusion of responsibility. People will walk by and not assist, especially if there are a lot of people present. Besides, there's no one in the bus station named "Somebody." If you find yourself in this situation make it impossible for a bystander to shirk responsibility. Pick on individuals and tell them what to do. "You wearing the green sweater and blue jeans, call 911!" "You wearing the polo shirt, love beads, and goatee, call the police!" "You wearing the three-piece gray-striped suit, call the fire department." By picking on individuals, you make it impossible for them to avoid responsibility. Responsibility lands on their shoulders, just like it did on ours in the restaurant.

Let me return to the Kitty Genovese murder for a moment. The idea that thirty eight people witnessed the murder and did nothing is wrong. It is an urban legend. The number of people who saw or heard enough to realize that Kitty was in mortal danger was five or six witnesses, not thirty eight. Only two clearly saw the murder and did nothing—a janitor in a building across the street and her next door neighbor. This neighbor was a lout and a coward. He opened his front door and saw her being stabbed. (He lived at the top of a flight of stairs and the murder occurred at the bottom.) He shut the door, called a friend, and climbed in fear out a back window.

One witness opened the window and yelled, "Leave that girl alone." This cry likely scared Moseley off for a while. At least two witnesses called the police. (This was in the days before there was a 9-1-1 hot line to the police station—the process in getting aide by phone proceeded much slower then.) And a neighbor named Sophie Farrar left her apartment and was with Kitty as she died.

An irony in this case is that Moseley was arrested several days later when a bystander saw him carrying a television set out a neighbor's apartment.

The next topic I'll like to cover in social psychology is *attitudes*. An attitude is defined as *an enduring set of thoughts, feelings, and evaluations about people, objects, or issues.* Every attitude has three components. These components are a *cognitive or belief component,* an *affective or feeling component,* and a *behavioral or action component.*

I have the attitude that vegetarianism is the preferred culinary lifestyle. I base this belief on nutritional information. I feel strongly about the issue—it saddens me how many cows are sent to the slaughterhouse. Behaviorally, I eat vegetables, I buy vegetables, and I hand out pamphlets recommending the vegetarian lifestyle on street corners.

I have the attitude that pro-choice should govern a woman's right to have a baby or not. I base this belief on American law. I feel strongly about the issue. I vote for candidates who are pro-choice.

Finally, I am for the death penalty. I base this belief on law and on religion. I feel strongly about the issue. I contribute to candidates who are for the death penalty.

People want to be *consistent* when it comes to the components of attitudes. The fact is, however, that the three components of attitudes are often inconsistent and *correlate with low predictability*. I might have a lot of beliefs about a topic and I might feel strongly about it, but do little behaviorally in support of my attitude. Conversely, I might have few beliefs about a topic and I might have no feelings one way or the other, but I might engage in proactive behaviors.

Correlations among the three components increase *when the attitudes are specific.* I usually vote Democratic, but I have no favorite in this election—it's not easy to predict who I'll vote for. I might vote Republican or write in a candidate. But in another election I really like Al Smith for governor. You can place a wager that I'll vote for Al Smith. I might even send him five dollars—I'm sure he'll appreciate the donation. I'm vaguely in favor of the death penalty—it's difficult to predict if I'll vote for a pro-death penalty candidate. I'm in favor of the death penalty for criminals who murder children. You can be sure who I'll vote for.

We acquire our attitudes in the ways we acquire any thought or behavior. We learn them through classical conditioning, through operant conditioning, and through imitation. There are strong pressures to conform to the attitudes of the group we happen to be in. And there are strong pressures to obey authorities. I suppose I should add that we can develop attitudes on our own. Sometimes we can think for ourselves. Sometimes we can resist the pressures to conform and to obey. Perhaps we come up with an idiosyncratic belief or with a divergent behavior. If we do, we can be sure that we will be consistent when expressing the three components of attitudes.

The next topic derives from attitudes, but it is so important we need to treat it separately. This is *cognitive dissonance*, a concept introduced into psychology in the 1950s by New York born psychologist Leon Festinger (1919-1984). It's amazing how many important psychologists were born in New York City. Maybe there's something in the drinking water that produces important psychologists.

Let me outline cognitive dissonance. People want to be consistent in their beliefs and their behaviors. Sometimes a conflict happens. One belief clashes with a second belief. Or our behaviors clash with our beliefs. In either case we are no longer consistent. Our beliefs and our behaviors are dissonant. We feel uncomfortable about the dissonance and we are motivated to become consistent. Often it's not easy to regain consistency by changing behaviors—it may not be possible to undo what we have done or to take back a behavior. We can become consistent by changing our beliefs. It's a lot easier to change beliefs than to undo behaviors.

Consider my previous examples. I believe in the vegetarian lifestyle, but I just ate a hamburger. I believe in pro-choice, but I just voted for a pro-life candidate. I believe in the death penalty, but I just spoke out against it in a particular case. In each of the three examples I experience dissonance—another word for dissonance is "inconsistency." I said one thing and did something else. I believed one thing and behaved in a way that clashed with my beliefs.

I can't undo the behaviors, but I can *justify* what I did and I can make exceptions. I can say to the effect that I prefer the vegetarian lifestyle, but a little meat every now and then never hurt anyone. I can say to the effect that I believe in pro-choice, but the pro-life candidate was, overall, the superior candidate in this election. I can say to the effect that I am for the death penalty, but in this case the facts weren't clear and we have to be careful not to execute an innocent person.

We can perceive the process of *justification* in one of the early experiments in cognitive dissonance. We can also see what happens when we can't justify what we did. In 1959 Festinger and Carlsmith required volunteers in their experiment to perform a boring and meaningless task—filling trays with spools and then removing the spools and starting over. After an hour passed the experimenter explained that they served as participants in a control group that received no special instructions to perform the task. They were told that members of an experimental group would perform the same task and would receive instructions that included the statement that the task would be enjoyable. The participants were then asked if they would tell a member of the experimental group that the task was enjoyable. In essence, they were asked to lie. Half the students were paid $1.00 to misrepresent the task. Half were paid $20.00 to misrepresent the task. Twenty dollars an hour was a princely amount in 1959. Twenty dollars an hour remains a princely amount in our time of economic woe.

After the students interacted with a member of the experimental group, they were asked to rate the task on a five point scale. One question asked whether they found the task enjoyable. Students who were paid $1.00 reported that they found the task more enjoyable than students who were paid $20.00. Another question asked whether they would be willing to participate in a second experiment. Students who were paid $1.00 indicated they would be more willing to repeat the experience than students who were paid $20.00.

Festinger and Carlsmith conjectured that the participants in the group that was paid $20.00 could justify their behavior. "I'm a happening person and the task that I just misrepresented to another student was boring and meaningless. Only a fool does something boring and meaningless. Only a fool recommends a boring and meaningless task. I was paid $20.00 to do this. I'm no fool. The experimenters are the fools for paying me so much." The group that was paid $1.00

couldn't justify their behavior and they couldn't undo their behavior. They could only adjust their beliefs. "I'm a happening person and the task that I just misrepresented to another student was boring and meaningless. Only a fool does something boring and meaningless. Only a fool recommends a boring and meaningless task. I was paid $1.00 to do this. I'm no fool. The task wasn't boring, the task wasn't meaningless. I rather like what I did."

We have to be careful not to rely too heavily on Festinger and Carlsmith's experiment. The average difference between the key survey questions—was the task enjoyable and would they be willing to repeat it?—was less than two points on the survey scale. There were only twenty participants in each group and the procedure may have been overly manipulative. It may have been obvious what the experiment was about. Eleven participants were dismissed from the experiment when they failed to cooperate or when they guessed the hypothesis.

Cognitive dissonance may underlie why people who undergo severe initiation rites bond with the organizations that put them through misery. A few years ago a study was done correlating the severity of hazing in fraternities and sororities at Rutgers University in beautiful New Jersey with the drop-out rates from such organizations. Commonsense might inform us that the more severe the hazing, the higher the drop-out rate. It's too much bother to join and it hurts too much. In fact, the reverse was found. The more severe the initiation, the lower the drop-out rate. The less severe the initiation, the higher the drop-out rate.

A cognitive dissonance explanation was offered to explain the correlation. It goes something like this. "I'm a dignified self-respecting person. This sorority is making me do something dangerous or difficult or foolish or time-consuming to join. Only a fool would do something dangerous or difficult or foolish or time-consuming. I'm no fool. What I'm doing isn't dangerous or difficult or foolish or time-consuming. I rather like what I'm doing. I value the sorority and wish to join it." The candidate is in much the same position as the people paid $1.00 to package and repackage spools of thread. It's difficult to justify one's behavior and impossible to undo it. It is possible to change one's beliefs to be consistent with one's behavior.

Individuals who undergo severe initiations rationalize what they did—the initiation wasn't so bad. They come to exaggerate the positive aspects of the group. They put a lot of time and effort into joining.

Maybe they even spent a lot of money. Individuals who undergo weak initiations have no need to rationalize what they did—there's nothing to rationalize. They tend not to value the organization. They didn't work very hard to join and they spent little in the way of time or money.

This kind of research suggests that if we want people to remain in a group and to value the group, we should make it difficult for them to join the group. If we make it too easy to join, there is no change in beliefs and no loyalty to the group. If we make things too easy, people don't value what they get. Making a goal difficult to attain makes the goal more attractive. The lesson for ladies is obvious—when a young man courts you, play hard to get. The harder you play, the more earnestly your young man will court you and the more he will value you.

Of course, there are other reasons besides cognitive dissonance why a person would work hard to join a particular group. Fraternities and sororities can be rank ordered in terms of prestige and power. Students on campus know which organizations have clubhouses in the penthouse and which have clubhouses in the basement. Students will endure severe initiations to be able to join the prestige organizations. Students may be willing to do dangerous or difficult or foolish or time-consuming behaviors in order to share in the privileges conferred by the first-tier organization. Members of the second-tier organizations lack such privileges.

Cognitive dissonance may play a role in the interpersonal aspects of self-efficacy and in why we like people to whom we provide reinforcements. Self-efficacy is the belief that we can perform successfully in particular situations. We prefer to feel efficacious. And other people like us when we make them feel efficacious.

You might remember the story I told in the personality lecture about the two men vying for the hand of the same lady. Both arranged sleigh rides to restaurants on the Boston Post Road. On both rides the horse's harness came loose. One man promptly fixed the harness and they were on the way. I'm sure he thought he impressed the lady's father. The second man claimed he didn't know how to fix the harness. The father had to fix it. I'm sure the father thought he impressed the suitor. When it came time to claim the lady's hand, the man who didn't know how to repair the harness won the courtship. I don't know what happened to the other man. I like to think he was able to rebound from the loss—maybe he found true love on another sleigh ride. I suggested the result was due to self-efficacy—the second young man made the father feel important. It may be the resolution of the story also has to do with cognitive dissonance.

Consider what might be going on in the father's mind as he tightens the harness. "I'm the senior citizen here. I shouldn't have to do physical labor when there's a younger man present. Young men are supposed to know how to tighten harnesses. I shouldn't have to do this, but I am. He's just standing over my shoulder watching what I do." At this point the father may be mighty aggravated. But he can't loosen the harness he just tightened—that would be counterproductive. He can't take back what he did. He can change his beliefs. "I'm in better shape than that young man and I'm more knowledgeable when it comes to horse drawn sleighs. Tightening a harness isn't hard work. It's is good exercise and it gives me a chance to work up an appetite."

The father can think ill of the young man. But if he thinks ill of him, why is he helping him? Why is he showing him what to do? Why is he teaching him the mechanics of tightening harnesses? He can change his beliefs and develop a favorable attitude about the young man. "Only a fool would let an incompetent man marry his daughter. I'm no fool. I'm a responsible father. This guy has a lot to learn and I'm the fellow to teach him. He'll make an excellent son-in-law."

I wonder if cognitive dissonance explains true love. A man thinks, "I wined her and I dined her. I waited hand and foot on her every whim. I was at her beck and call. I spent a fortune courting her. I suffered abuse to my self-esteem because of her. I made a fool of myself in front of other people. How can I not love her?"

Cognitive dissonance opens up an important avenue of producing attitude change. *If we want to change people's attitudes, we need to get them to act in ways that clash with their beliefs.* Remember that it's often difficult to undo behavior—that's me on camera, that's my handwriting on the petition, that's my name on the check. It's easier to adjust one's beliefs. If we want to change people's attitudes, we need to get them to experience cognitive dissonance.

If I wanted to change your vegetarian lifestyle I need to get you to eat a slice of meat. It needn't be flank steak—that's asking for too much at the outset. It can be the tiny clot of meat at the end of my fork. Maybe I can start with chicken gravy. Later, I can remind you that you ate meat and of not being a true vegetarian. You can't disagree—everyone at the table saw you swallow.

If you're pro-choice and I want to nudge you to the pro-life position, I need to get you to do something in support of the pro-life position. It needn't be anything dramatic. Maybe I can ask you to watch a program advancing the pro-life position. Maybe I can ask you to sign a petition in support of a pro-life candidate. Maybe I can invite you to accompany me to a pro-life rally. Later, I can remind you that you attended a pro-life rally. You can't disagree—you were caught on film.

I have to do the same about changing your attitude toward the death penalty. You're for the death penalty, so I need to get you to act in a way that clashes with your beliefs. Maybe I can ask you to sign a petition requesting a stay of execution for a particular criminal. Maybe I can get you to read literature describing in gruesome detail the particulars of executing a prisoner. Maybe I get you to watch a movie about a condemned man—maybe a condemned man who was innocent of the crime he was put to death for. Later, I can remind you that you watched the movie. You can't disagree—you have the movie stub in your pocket and butter stains on your blouse.

To change attitudes we must get people to perform a behavior that clashes with their beliefs. We must get people to stand up and do something different. People stand up for what they believe in and people believe what they stand up for. Permit me to repeat the mighty magic of cognitive dissonance—people believe what they stand up for even if they didn't believe it before they stood up. People want to be consistent. If I'm standing up for something, I must believe it.

I have to be careful to get you to willingly perform the behavior. If you feel you are being forced to perform a behavior you would ordinarily not perform, you don't feel dissonance. The fact that I'm forcing you to do something provides justification for performing the behavior. You think, "I'm not inconsistent—I'm being forced to do something."

The change in behavior need not be profound or dramatic. Salespeople have the "free sample" and the "foot-in-the-door" techniques. I ask you to do something minor at the outset and I slowly escalate the requests. I might ask you to put a stamp on the envelop contributing to a pro-life candidate. The next time I might ask you to walk to the mailbox and drop the letter in. The next time I might ask you to lick the envelope. The next time I might ask you to write the address. The next time I might ask you to read the letter. The next time I might ask you to proofread the letter. The next time I might ask you to write the letter. By this time, you're probably in support of the pro-life position.

The last topic we cover in social psychology is *prejudice*. Harry Stack Sullivan observed that selective inattention covers the world. (Selective inattention is the concept that people fail to notice things that make them anxious.) Well, prejudice makes selective inattention look like an umbrella in a blizzard. It is a fact of life that prejudice remains so sadly vibrant in the twenty-first century. We're still polarized into groups. We're still mercilessly at one another's throats. You'd think we'd learn differently, but we never do.

We have our disgraceful history of slavery and racial hatred in the United States. Currently, we see how the issue of immigration has bedeviled Americans. I grew up in a working class city that was decidedly anti-Latino. I lived in another city where there was a large Indian population. There were two delicatessens in the neighborhood. One was owned by a dark-skinned Indian. The other was owned by a light-skinned Indian. It never failed that the one owner disparaged the personality, cleanliness, and work habits of the other owner.

It's not only America where we see the effects of prejudice. There are riots in my ancestral home of Ireland over a battle fought a thousand years ago. In my other ancestral home of Lithuania I heard the Baltic tour guide disparage Slavs, who she claimed were lazy and unpatriotic.

It's not only in my ancestral homes. Consider the bloodbath we unleashed in Iraq where Shiites massacre Sunnis and vice versa. Consider the bloodbath in Bosnia in the 1990s, when Serbs engaged in an "ethnic cleansing" of Muslims. Consider the bloodbath in Rwanda, where Hutu tribesmen massacred nearly a million Tutsis in one month. Consider the bloodbath in Cambodia where the communist regime of Pol Pot massacred more than two million people. Consider the organized massacre of Jews, gays, gypsies, Communists, and Jehovah Witnesses by the Nazis in the Holocaust. Before that, consider the slaughter of Armenians by the Turks. The list is nauseating—they are not numbers I'm describing, but human lives, lives like yours and mine.

Prejudice goes on all the time and virtually in every place. Prejudice must be the Horseman left out of the *Book of Revelation*.

Social psychology defines *prejudice as an unjustifiable negative attitude directed toward a group*. We don't usually speak of being prejudiced toward an individual, although the individual may be representative of a group. And we don't usually speak of prejudice as being something positive. We sometimes use the word in a favorable sense, as in "I'm prejudiced toward leggy blondes," but that's not really correct in the sense social psychologists use the term.

Attitudes have three components, as you know. The belief component in prejudice involves *stereotypes*, which are overly simple generalizations about a group. So we say a particular group is greedy or lazy. A danger with stereotyping is that the people who hold stereotypes may come to believe something untrue about a group. They may come to believe something that drives wedges between groups. And they may come to believe something based on an exaggerated or unusual behavior not otherwise common to the prejudiced group. It may be something they read in the paper or viewed on the nightly newscast. Another danger with stereotyping is that the people stereotyped may come to believe what others say about them. They may come to believe their group is greedy or lazy.

The feeling components involve *fear* and *hostility*. I don't like a particular group. I'm on my guard when one of them enters a room. In the movie *Remember the Titans*, a film about a racially integrated football team in Virginia, the injured white player says something insightful to his new-found black friend. He says, "I hated you because I was afraid of you."

The behavioral component involves *avoidance* and *discrimination*. It may also involve *disparagement*, although not usually to people's faces.

Prejudice is an exceedingly complex phenomenon. The stork drops us into a world that is already established. We are born into a social-cultural milieu that includes prejudices in the same way it includes religious, political, economic, scientific, and technological realities. I'm handed prejudices in the same way I'm handed political beliefs or church doctrines. For that matter, I'm handed prejudices in the way I'm handed a textbook of general psychology or some other subject. Slavery was more than a century old when the Civil War started. The people of the South were born into it, like they were born into a particular style of architecture or to a particular diet.

We are born into societies where prejudice is an organized phenomenon. Economically, consider the use of minorities as sources of labor. This goes on today and not only with the immigrants who enter America, but across the globe. The ideas of prejudice are in place. The historical memories are in place. So are many of the slang words and phrases we carelessly use. We receive considerable *positive reinforcement* for repeating these ideas and words. We may be severely *punished*— ostracized or worse—for disagreeing with such ideas or for associating with the despised group. God forbid we should say a kind word on their behalf. God forbid we should take their side or defend them. In the Old South the only people whites disliked more than blacks were white people who fraternized with black people.

We may exhibit prejudice because we *conform* to a particular group. And we may exhibit prejudice because we *obey* an authority figure. This figure may be a teacher or a scientist or a political figure. This figure may also be a parent who makes derogatory references about particular groups.

The obvious example is Nazi Germany—Nazi Germany is the obvious example for just about everything negative. *Der Fuhrer* told Germans who stabbed Germany in the back in World War One and what they can do about it. Church leaders and creative artists concurred with *Der Fuhrer*. So did scientists, who proved the inferiority of certain groups compared to the superior Aryans. So did school teachers in classrooms. So did parents at the dinner tables. To believe otherwise was to make yourself an exception. Becoming an exception in a land of concentration camps was not an enviable choice.

Prejudice is tied into the social fabric of our beings. We exhibit *ethnocentrism*, which is *the belief that our group is superior to all other groups*. I suppose I observed ethnocentrism in the delicatessens where I bought my coffee and Danish. We gravitate toward specific groups and alliances. We gravitate toward people who look like us and dress like us and say the same things we say. Banding together, we make the *fundamental attribution error* in an interesting way. We overestimate the similarity of the personalities and beliefs of the members in our group. And we overestimate the differences between our group and the personalities and attitudes of members of other, supposedly inferior, groups.

We get information how to live and how to advance our welfare by being in a group. We get self-esteem by being in a group. And we get self-esteem by disparaging other groups. "We're not like those greedy so-and-so's." "We're not like those lazy so-and-so's." We obtain explanations for our problems by *scapegoating*. This is *blaming our problems on a weaker group*. Scapegoating goes back to Biblical times when the Hebrews pinned their woes on a goat and chased the goat out of the village, where it was promptly consumed by predators. Today in America we blame immigrants for our woes. Our economy is bad—the immigrants are to blame. Our school system is failing—the immigrants are to blame. Our taxes are going up—the immigrants are to blame. The crime rate is going up—the immigrants are to blame. It's raining—the immigrants are to blame.

Prejudice is rooted in the social fabric of our beings. In the 1950s Sherif and Sherif—that's Muzafer Sherif, not Omar, and his wife Carolyn—performed a series of experiments in a summer camp for eleven-and-twelve-year old boys. In one experiment they randomly selected boys to be in one of two groups—the "Eagles" or the "Rattlers." None of the boys knew one another before arriving at the camp. Solidarity was developed through competition between the two groups. It didn't take long for each group to coalesce. In a short time the boys bonded to such an extent that an insult to one Eagle was an insult directed at all Eagles. A slight to one Rattler was a slight directed at all Rattlers.

We might notice what happens in times of crises—the group becomes more polarized and more cohesive. People in the conservative South and Midwest thought New Yorkers were slick Yankees and city sophisticates of the worst ilk. Then the Twin Towers fell. People from the conservative South and Midwest drove cross country to help. Remember what happened when we invaded Iraq. Many people were against the war, but as soon as the troops came under fire everyone drew together and the criticism became muted.

I'll like to mention one more social psychological principle that relates to prejudice. This is the *self-fulfilling prophecy*. You may have encountered this term in another course, but social psychologists mean something different than the use of the term in philosophy or personality psychology. In the self-fulfilling prophecy we *cause people to act in particular ways and then we blame them for acting in those ways.*

We see the self-fulfilling prophecy in parties and in taverns where an alcoholic becomes inebriated. Often, people will see to it that an alcoholic's glass is kept full. They'll pour drinks freely. Once he becomes blotto, they laugh at him and call him derogatory names. "See, he's a drunk." But who kept pouring the drinks?

A particularly clear example of the self-fulfilling prophecy occurs in the movie *Betrayed*. Tom Berenger plays a right-wing fanatic and Debra Winger plays a FBI agent who infiltrates his posse. It's not a good movie. If you paid to see it, you'd demand your money back. But there is one outstanding scene. Berenger's posse shanghais an elderly black man. They take him into the swamp and give him a gun and a half hour head start. If he can make it out of the bayou, he can live. If he can't, well, so much the better. They're playing "the most dangerous game" of hunting a human being. Of course, they catch up to the old man and the Berenger character kills him in cold blood. Winger's character screams, "Why did you kill that man?" Berenger answers, "We had to. He had a gun." But who gave the man the gun?

We may think a movie is far removed from social issues and prejudices, but the principle of the self-fulfilling prophecy is the same. The political, economic, and historical process keeps people in subjugation and blames the people for being subjugated. The process makes it impossible for people to advance out of poverty. The process proceeds to make the fundamental attribution error of accusing the people of not being able to climb up the socioeconomic ladder.

When I say "the process" I don't particularly mean what you and I do. I admit to being a sinner and poor, so I count myself among the unfortunates. And I don't refer to any specific dominant group or to a conspiracy in the halls of power. I refer to the structure of society and to the way our culture is organized. This has to do with history and with the way things worked out or didn't work out in the past. We are the recipients and the successors of what the people of the past did or did not do. This point is a fundamental social psychological principle. Our lives are connected not only with one another in the here and now. Our lives are connected with the people of the past. This may sound like a gloomy situation, but it's not. When we realize the connectedness of our lives we can appreciate the responsibilities we have to the people who come after us. We're connected with them as well. We have a responsibility to make the right choices and to lay out the right paths so the people of the future will live less burdened lives. I think we see that now with the changing attitudes toward race and toward homosexuality and gender issues and toward the environment. But we don't see it in enough topics or across a vaster scale. The fact that the people of the past failed is no reason why we have to return the favor.

Thank you.

TIPS TO STUDENTS ~
How to Take a Multiple-Choice Quiz

Like studying, test taking is a skill. Some students study intensely and then sabotage themselves by poor test-taking habits. They don't know how to take a quiz or they take it in an inappropriate manner and their grade suffers. They don't get the grade their efforts merit. If students know how to take a quiz—and if they study, of course—they maximize their performance and are more likely to obtain high grades. Here are a few tips on how to take a multiple-choice quiz.

Read the questions carefully. *Don't change the wording of the questions.* It's a common mistake to read a question and then to try to figure out what the question "really means." (Some students convince themselves that the quiz is "tricky." Professors rarely start out to make a quiz tricky—that happens by mischance.) In psychology there are a number of concepts that are similar and opposite—for example, proactive and retroactive interference and intrinsic and extrinsic motivation. It's easy to change one into the other and to answer a different question. Be careful to answer precisely what is asked.

Read all four choices, a), b), c), and d). Read all four even if you believe a) or b) is the answer. *Be careful not to add choices.* You do not need to retrieve the entire chapter to answer a specific question. Do not complicate the question more than it is. Limit yourself to the choices on the quiz.

This is the key to taking a multiple-choice quiz—if you studied, *do not select what does not look familiar.* If you studied, do not select what you don't recognize. Multiple-choice quizzes are tests of recognition retrieval. Do not turn the quiz into a test of recall retrieval. The answer is not in your head—stop thinking mental. The answer is on the paper in front of you. The answer is staring you in the face and crying, "Select me! Select me!" You can practically see the parenthesis squiggling in exasperation. Your task is not to drop a tow line into the murky sea of semantic memory. Your task is to recognize the choice on the paper.

Many students lack self-confidence in their study habits and feel that they did not study enough. They see a choice on the quiz that they do not recognize. They don't remember seeing the choice in the book. They don't remember hearing it in the lecture. They mistakenly think, "This must be the choice," and they select it. This is exactly opposite to how students should proceed. *Never select a choice you don't recognize.*

Answer all choices. If you fail to answer a question, it will be marked wrong. Before handing in the quiz, double check that you answered everything.

If you get absolutely stuck on a question, try to eliminate one or two of the choices. If you can eliminate two choices, it's fifty/fifty you'll get the right answer by picking one of the remaining two choices randomly. Don't try to prove how a choice fits the question. Rather, *try to disprove and eliminate choices.* Alternately, you can place a mark next to the question and return to it after you've answered the rest of the quiz. Sometimes the answer can be retrieved by looking at other questions later in the quiz.

You can write on the quiz. Some students like to jot down acronyms and mnemonics to keep their memories fresh.

The evidence is mixed on what actually happens, but if you studied *it is not recommended changing answers.* It's not recommended changing answers if you are guessing that your initial response is wrong. Initial responses are frequently correct in tests of recognition memory. Students get second thoughts and argue themselves out of the correct answer. Of course, you can change answers if you like. This is America and we are at liberty to change any answer on any quiz. This is what democracy is all about—the right to change answers. We're bestowing that right on school children across the globe. Democracy is on the march. So is the right to change answers.

Lecture Six ~
Psychological Disorders

Being perfectly normal myself, I find it difficult to lecture on psychological disorders. It is a topic I have no familiarity with. Despite this fortuitous shortcoming, I suppose I have to make the effort for the sake of our completing this voyage of intellectual discovery.

Psychological disorder implies that we have a standard of *psychological order*. Alas, we don't. *Abnormal behavior* implies that we have a notion of what constitutes *normal behavior*. Equally alas, we don't.

Normal behavior in the sense of *average behavior* or *what everyone does* is not an acceptable standard for identifying abnormal behavior. People who exhibit abnormal behavior may be statistically infrequent. So are geniuses. We wouldn't say geniuses are abnormal in the same way we say schizophrenics are abnormal.

What everyone does in a particular society cannot constitute a standard for defining abnormality for another reason. Abnormal behavior may constitute normality in entire societies. In Nazi Germany hatred and violence and extreme prejudice were the norm. Compassion and pacifism and tolerance were the exceptions. These attitudes constituted abnormalities in 1930s Germany. These attitudes could get people sent to concentration camps.

Normal and abnormal behavior are *culturally defined*. What constitutes normal behavior at one time and place can transform into abnormal behavior at another time and place. Consider that smoking was once considered acceptable. When I was in college we could smoke in class. We now regard smoking as a dangerous and self-destructive behavior. You have to stand outside buildings to smoke. In the Old

South it was considered the norm for one group of people to own another group of people. We now recognize slavery as an abhorrent evil. The reverse is also true. What constitutes abnormal behavior at one time and place can transform into normal behavior at another time and place. Homosexuality was once considered a psychological disorder. It no longer is. Outside the Bible Belt gay people are treated with the same largess as straight people. Maybe they're treated with same largess inside the Bible Belt as well, but I don't live there and I can't say for sure.

Another approach is to use *personal distress* as the standard for defining abnormal behavior. If people are personally distressed and discomforted by their thoughts and behaviors, then they can be considered psychologically disordered. This is, at best, a partial approach to defining abnormality. If people are distressed by what they think and do, they certainly require assistance. However, there are categories of disorder in which people demonstrate abnormal behavior and suffer little or no personal distress. There's the lame joke about a "problem drinker." He has no problem drinking. Everyone else has a problem with his drinking. And there are personality disorders such as antisocial personalities who can be great nuisances to other people and experience no personal qualms about the mayhem they produce.

Another approach is to use *the ability to function in society* as the standard of normal and abnormal behavior. If a person can hold a job, support a family, and serve as a model citizen, then he or she is normal. This approach is as ineffective as the previous approaches. In Nazi Germany the people who advanced their careers and showed the most efficiency were often the most hateful, bigoted, and intolerant individuals. Many people with certifiable disorders function successfully. The tall buildings of New York are crammed with "functioning alcoholics." The tall buildings are filled with anxious and depressed people and with people demonstrating personality disorders. And failure to succeed in a society as complex and stressful as our own is no indicator that there's anything the matter with a person.

In the first lecture I stated that psychological disorders are studied by the subfield of *clinical psychology*. Clinical psychologists engage in research to uncover the causes of psychological disorders. They provide various types of psychotherapies. They also engage in research that assesses the efficacy of these types of psychotherapies. There is a medical specialty called *psychiatry* that also studies the causes and treatments of psychological disorders. Psychiatrists are medical doctors. They go to medical school. They were put on earth to prescribe medicines. Clinical psychologists are doctors of philosophy. They go to graduate school. They do not prescribe medicine. They would like to, but that hasn't happened yet on a nationwide scale, which is probably a good thing.

Clinical psychologists and psychiatrists take two approaches in defining psychological disorder. The first approach is theoretical. The second approach is pragmatic and based on differential diagnosis.

In the first lecture I outlined seven perspectives that orient us to the kind of data we should seek to obtain in answering psychological questions. They are the neuroscience, behavioral, cognitive, psychodynamic, social cultural, behavior genetics, and evolutionary perspectives. As we near port and prepare to disembark and go our separate ways, we can revisit these perspectives. Each of them suggests where we should look for the causes and, ultimately, for the treatments of psychological disorders.

The *neuroscience perspective* suggests that we should study the brain if we want to identify the causes of psychological disorders. The brain is the origin of thoughts, emotions, and behaviors. If the brain becomes damaged or diseased, thoughts, emotions, and behaviors may change in such a way as to get called "disordered" and "abnormal."

In Europe in the eighteenth century disordered people were shackled and brutalized and treated as freaks. They were imprisoned and put in circuses and in side shows. The medical treatment of disordered people commenced as a corrective to these barbaric practices. The medical approach suggested that disordered people should be treated in a humane manner. They were not curiosities to be laughed at. They were sick people. In the same way that hearts and kidneys and livers become sick, the brain can become sick.

In the late nineteenth and early twentieth centuries the *medical model* of psychological disorder developed within psychiatry. The medical model was based on *paresis*, the third and terminal phase of the venereal disease syphilis. There was no cure for syphilis at that time period—this was before antibodies were discovered. People suffering paresis develop brain damage and exhibit a medley of abnormal behaviors. They can hallucinate and become emotionally agitated and highly anxious and confused in their thinking. All these symptoms depend on brain damage. And in this case the brain damage depends on a germ. The implication was clear. Psychological disorder is caused by brain damage and brain damage—at least in the case of paresis—is caused by a germ. The search was on. Schizophrenia, depression, anxiety, the rest of them—it was expected that these disorders would be shown to be caused by actual brain damage and by germs. As the years rolled on, the search for germs abated. The search for brain damage continued, although the emphasis shifted after 1950 to the neurotransmitters and to genetics. The search continues.

The neuroscience perspective—the medical model—is the most prominent and powerful perspective when it comes to psychological disorders. It provides the terminology of psychological disorder—the very term *mental disorder* suggests that psychological disorders are akin to physical illnesses. If we become psychologically disordered, we go to a medical doctor. The doctor prescribes medicines. If we are severely disordered, we may become patients in the psych ward of a general hospital or in the ward of a "mental hospital." There use to be a mental hospital in the Bronx near the Hutchinson River Parkway. "Bronx State" it was called. It was a huge grim building and one of the scariest places on earth. I don't know if it's still there—the hospital, that is, not the Bronx. I'm sure I would have heard if the Bronx was no longer there.

Three perspectives are closely linked to psychology. These are the behavioral, cognitive, and psychodynamic perspectives.

The *behavioral perspective* originated in the psychology of learning. It became a vibrant and important field after World War Two, although behavioral interventions to reduce fears occurred as far back as the 1920s. The behavioral perspective fathered such fields as *behavior modification*, which was based on B. F. Skinner's research in operant conditioning, and *behavior therapy*, which was a wider approach based both on operant conditioning and on classical conditioning. The behavior perspective prefers to focus on situational factors rather than on personality factors, specifically on the reinforcements and punishments a person receives. Reinforcements and punishments are considered the determining factors whether a person exhibits ordered or disordered behavior.

The *cognitive perspective* applied to psychological disorder is a somewhat later development. Two men associated with the cognitive perspective are Aaron Beck and Albert Ellis. Until he got booted out in his old age for possible financial shenanigans, Ellis founded and ran a clinic uptown in your country. The idea with the cognitive perspective is that psychologically disordered people engage in negative and self-defeating patterns of thinking. These patterns sabotage behavior and interpersonal relationships. The cognitive approach has become important in the treatment of depression and it is frequently combined with the behavioral perspective.

The *psychodynamic perspective* is an old one in psychology, going back to Sigmund Freud and others in the 1880s. This perspective suggests that we should study the personalities and the unconscious minds of disordered individuals. This perspective offers the stereotype of a psychotherapist sitting behind a client—I almost said "patient," which would be a medical term—who's lying on a couch and talking about his or her dreams.

The *social-cultural perspective* emphasizes relationships and cultural factors as the causes of psychological disorders. Individuals are not disordered. Relationships are disordered. Families are disordered. Societies are disordered—think Nazi Germany, again. We see the relevance of the social-cultural perspective in the changes in attitudes that occur in societies over time—think of slave ownership and of homosexuality. We also see the relevance of this perspective in *family therapy*. A child may be showing particular *symptoms*—another medical term—of a particular disorder, but the parents are involved in the origin and development of the disorder just as much as the child. The focus of treatment is not on the isolated child, but on the inter-connected family. It's the family that's messed up.

Like the neuroscience perspective, the *behavior genetics perspective* is especially powerful in our time. The search is on for the genes—for the pattern of genes—that in interaction with the environment give rise to psychological disorders. The belief is that there is a genetic predisposition to psychological disorder in the same manner that there is a genetic predisposition to heart disease and to lung disease.

There is an interesting variant of behavior genetics that relates this predisposition to stress. If stress becomes overwhelming, individuals so predisposed breakdown psychologically. Individuals not so predisposed breakdown in other ways—maybe with digestive problems or with rashes or with headaches. Two implications of this variant are relevant. If individuals so predisposed are in a stress-free environment, they will tend not to experience psychological problems. And psychotherapy may be facilitated when stress is reduced. The person gets better when stress is reduced.

I realize I'm using the term "predisposition" loosely. There's a lot of research going into identifying predispositions. When it comes to depression, for example, several gene patterns have been identified that may serve as predispositions. These patterns tend to run in families, so researchers need to control for the possibility that depression is learned or based on environmental events. None of these genetic patterns accounts for the majority of cases of depression. It will likely be the case that there are multiple genetic routes to the same pattern of symptoms.

I'm sure it exists, but I can't for the life of me see how the *evolutionary perspective* applies to the study of psychological disorders. Perhaps the panicky reaction middle-aged women make to the appearance of mice demonstrates this perspective.

The pragmatic or *differential diagnosis* approach to psychological disorder avoids theories. It tries to develop a symptom-based approach to disorders. It defines specific disorders by listing precisely stated symptoms that occur together. These symptoms are strongly positively correlated. They indicate particular disorders or *syndromes* that presumably can be demarcated one from the other. The causes of the syndromes are not stated in this approach. Nor is there a focus on treatment.

Each symptom or syndrome is defined in terms of duration. To be described as suffering a particular disorder, a person must exhibit the relevant symptom for a precisely stated period of time.

The complete catalog of currently defined—of the currently recognized—psychological disorders is found in a book entitled *Diagnostic and Statistical Manual of the American Psychiatric Association.* Fortunately for the muscles in our writing hands, the abbreviation DSM is used.

There have been six versions of the DSM. The first appeared in 1952—DSM I. The most recent was published in May, 2013—DSM 5. (Unlike its predecessors, DSM 5 is identified with a number and not with a Roman numeral.) DSM I listed 106 disorders. DSM 5 lists over 300 disorders. Either we're getting sicker, a possibility that can't be dismissed, or psychiatric committees are getting better at drumming up grounds for business, a possibility that also can't be dismissed.

There are benefits in the use of the DSM. There are also problems.

One benefit provided by the DSM is the facilitation of research. Incredible as this sounds, there were no national or professional standards of diagnosis before the DSM was introduced. Every therapist of whatever experience and competence was free to use his or her own standards. There was little agreement over what constituted a disorder and over who qualified to be duly diagnosed. The same people could be diagnosed differently in different cities—this was differential diagnosis at its worst. A person could be bipolar in New York and schizo-affective in San Francisco. Another person could be obsessive compulsive in San Antonio and agoraphobic in Chicago. This chaotic situation made research impossible, since samples could not be equated. Researchers could not be certain they were speaking of the same disorder when they said their samples consisted of individuals diagnosed with a particular disorder.

The DSM is not a perfect system, but it inspires more confidence that samples consist of the same categories of disordered individuals. We have greater confidence that a person diagnosed with a particular disorder on the East Coast will be diagnosed with the same disorder on the West Coast.

The DSM is also beneficial in that it is necessary for insurance purposes. Insurance companies pay for psychotherapy—for a few sessions, anyway—and for psychiatric drugs, which can be pricey. As with physical ailments, psychiatrists are required to define the person's disorder and outline the course of treatment. Psychotherapy and medication are expensive and it helps if the person can pass some of the costs to health plans.

The DSM has problems as well as benefits. Perhaps it has more problems than benefits. Some critics feel these problems are insolvable.

Many of the disorders described in the DSM are not like physical diseases. They are psychiatric constructions created by the vote of committees. For example, in the early 1970s the American Psychiatric Association voted to remove homosexuality from the DSM, unless the person is discomforted by his or her orientation. The vote was 5,854 to remove homosexuality and 3,810 to keep it in DSM II. In a manner of speaking, psychiatrists outed homosexuality. I am not making those numbers up, by the way. That's the actual vote count.

This is not how it's done in other areas of medicine. The reason why psychiatrists vote to retain or to oust disorders is that there are very few disorders in the DSM that have biological markers, such as are found in diseases like diabetes and high blood pressure and in other medical conditions.

The use of ballots to identify disorders leads to the strange situation in which disorders come and go from versions of the DSM. Homosexuality is gone from DSM II. Asperger's Syndrome, a type of autism, is gone from DSM 5. Hoarding is in DSM 5. So is hypersexual disorder, which figures.

Another problem with respect to differential diagnosis is that the various disorders can blend into one another. It is not easy to demarcate one disorder from another. The same set of behaviors can be described as different conditions—is it anxiety or is it depression? Is it both anxiety and depression? To further complicate things, a person may drift from one disorder into another. For example, obsessions and compulsions may mask schizophrenia. The person uses obsessions and compulsions to control schizophrenic thoughts.

Critics have pointed out that the editions of the DSM have turned normal human experiences into medical maladies. A temper tantrum has become "disruptive mood dysregulative disorder." Rage has become "intermittent explosive disorder." Grief, shyness, loneliness, to name three, have been turned into disorders. So has the emotional response following traumatic experiences. These experiences now require treatment. In former decades treatment meant talking to a short guy with a goatee and an East European accent. In our time treatment means swallowing medications.

There's another problem with the DSM. This is the problem of labeling. There's a danger that the person will take the diagnosis to heart. "I am schizophrenic." "I am obsessive compulsive." "I am bipolar." These labels are ugly words representing ugly fates. Maybe I should have said "different fates." It's not easy to go through life as schizophrenic or as obsessive compulsive or as bipolar.

A collateral danger is that people will start to treat individuals as the label. They interpret everything the person does in accordance with the label. "See what the person's doing," they say. "The behavior proves the person is crazy." Perfectly ordinary behavior may be interpreted as symptomatic of a disorder and not as what it is—perfectly ordinary behavior. By the same token, perfectly odd behavior may be interpreted as normal if a person is judged not to be disordered.

The label may or may not be valid. Let's say for the sake of argument that it is. The person is schizophrenic. The person is obsessive compulsive. The person is bipolar. But the person is a lot more than the label. Humans are so complicated we cannot be defined by a label—by a single word, for God's sake. Is that all the person is? Schizophrenic? Obsessive compulsive? Bipolar? Of course, that's not all the person is.

I'm not only your teacher, I'm your friend. Let me give you friendly advice. It's rather important advice. If you ever experienced a psychological crises at some point in your life or if you were ever labeled as "psychologically disordered something or other," never tell anyone. There is more prejudice directed against former mental patients than against any other group. Let management find out that you were once labeled and your career has reached a dead end. Let the tenant review committee find out you were once labeled and you won't get the lease to the condo. Let the happening person at the club find out you were once labeled and you're spending the rest of the night alone.

I'm not sure why this prejudice exists. It doesn't exist for physical maladies and the neuroscience model teaches that psychological disorders are diseases of the brain. It may be that people are unsure how to act in the presence of a one-time psychologically disordered person. It may be that people expect the formerly psychologically disordered person to do something odd or dangerous. And there may be a feeling that the formerly psychologically disordered person is unpredictable and that he or she may relapse.

As I keep telling everyone, I'm perfectly normal and have no personal familiarity with psychological disorders. I try to understand psychological disorders in the following manner. Psychological disorders are *exaggerations* of normal behavior. Psychological disorders are *caricatures* of normal behavior. Disordered thoughts and behaviors are more intense than ordered thoughts and behaviors. Disordered thoughts and behaviors are more persistent and less amenable to change or to correction than ordered thoughts and behaviors. People who exhibit psychological disorders show a difference in degree and not in kind. They don't exhibit anything inherently different than what normal people exhibit. Maybe they show more of a particular behavior or psychological process. Maybe they show less. But the behavior or psychological process is part and parcel of what so-called normal people exhibit.

Since the difference between ordered and disordered behavior is one of degree and not of kind, it follows that psychologically disordered people are no different than we are—than I am, at any rate. The reverse is also true. We're no different than they are. If we keep this in mind, we may lose some of the fears and prejudices that complicate our interactions. If we emphasize similarities rather than differences, the aura of strangeness fades.

I'm going to outline four categories of psychological disorders. These categories are anxiety disorders, mood disorders, personality disorders, and thought disorders. Before I do, I'll like to address a final and rather important issue involving differential diagnosis. This is the issue between organic disorders and functional disorders.

Organic disorders, or organic brain disorders, are disorders that involve brain disease or damage. In the category of disease we would find paresis, which started the medical model rolling. In the category of damage we would find Alzheimer's and other forms of dementia. The idea with organic disorders is that there is something demonstrably wrong with the brain.

Functional disorders are disorders that involve no demonstrable brain disease or damage. What would we find as examples of functional disorders? Other than the personality disorders, this is a tricky question in an age dominated by the neuroscience perspective. Whether or not the brain has been shown to be diseased or damaged, virtually every disorder in the DSM has a pill jiggling in a thimble. As I mentioned at the outset of this intellectual voyage, we live in a time in which pills are reputed to cure all our ailments. Pills are reputed to cure conditions that may not even be ailments. I'm sure pills help to ameliorate many difficult conditions. Pills may give afflicted people second chances to get on with their lives. But we have to be careful with this excessive reliance on pills. We have to be on our guard as *educated consumers of research*. Research that shows that a particular medication doesn't work is rarely published. Negative results go into the paper shredder rather than into print. And we rarely know the proportion of positive results to negative results in pharmacological research. It is one thing if three out of three studies show the effectiveness of a particular pill. It is quite another thing if three out of ten studies show the effectiveness of a pill.

The three positive studies are published and the seven negative studies are placed on a barge and towed to the land of oblivion.

As I pointed out in the lecture on methodology, we need to know a lot before we say that a particular pill—or a particular treatment—works to cure a disorder. We need to know the percentage of people who improve taking a particular pill. We need to know the percentage of people who do not get better taking this pill. We need to know the percentage of people who get better taking a different pill or no pill. And we need to know the percentage of people who do not get better taking a different pill or no pill. That's a lot of information to accumulate and interpret.

The issue with respect to differential diagnosis is this. If a disorder is truly organic, engaging in verbal psychotherapy won't work. At best, talking about one's condition may serve to provide comfort and reassurance. If a disorder has not been shown to be organic, then we may not want to saturate our brains with medications or with the more intrusive methods that have been applied in the horrendously bleak history of psychiatry.

The first category of psychological disorders is *anxiety disorders*. These disorders are characterized by—you guessed it—the presence of anxiety. Anxiety means exactly what you think it means. It's that uneasy, nervous, and shuddery feeling that feels like fear. It's that feeling of unease and apprehension that comes upon us. We've all experienced anxiety. People who get diagnosed with an anxiety disorder experience these states more intensely and for longer periods. They feel these states in inappropriate situations and in innocuous situations. And they start to live their lives around the experience of anxiety. I should say they start to live their lives around avoiding the experience of anxiety. The anxiety is an exaggeration of normal anxiety. The behavior is a caricature of the ordinary response to anxiety.

There are a number of anxiety disorders. I'll mention two—phobic disorder and post-traumatic stress disorder.

Phobic disorder—phobia—is an intense irrational fear of a specific object or situation. The intensity of the anxiety is out of all proportion to the threat posed. The irrational element lies in the fact that the person has never had a bad experience with the object or situation. To count as a disorder, the phobia has to be experienced for a minimum of six months.

There are long lists of phobias, many with unpronounceable Greek or Latin names. There's a fear of sharp objects—aichmophobia. There's a fear of heights—acrophobia. There's a fear of enclosed places—claustrophobia. There's a fear of being buried alive—taphophobia. This fear was common in the days before embalming. There's a fear of open spaces—agoraphobia. There's a fear of cats—ailurophobia. There's a fear of dogs—cynophobia. There's a fear of fire—pyrophobia. There's a fear of one's wife—uxoriphobia. I suppose uxoriphobia may not be irrational in some marriages.

This can go one all afternoon, so let's stop and pick fear of sharp objects as a typical phobia—*aichmophobia*. It makes sense to fear sharp objects. We can chop a fingertip off if we're not careful dicing a salad. We can stab our feet if a knife slips out of our hand with the blade end pointed forward. We can disembowel ourselves with a butter knife if we slip on a scatter rug. But individuals with a phobia of sharp objects have rarely stabbed themselves. Phobic individuals experience intense anxiety when they see sharp objects. They start to live their lives to avoid sharp objects. They don't have knives in their homes. They close their eyes when walking through the cutlery aisle in Macy's Cellar. They don't carry switchblades for protection. They ask the server not to include knives with the silverware.

Consider the fear of heights—*acrophobia*. It makes sense to fear heights. If we fall out the window, we'll be donning ethereal wings the moment we hit the sidewalk. Or so we like to think. People with a phobia about heights have never fallen out windows. They experience intense anxiety when they're above the ground floor. They start to live their lives to avoid being above the ground floor. They can't work in a skyscraper—one with windows, anyway. They can't take a class in a room with windows above ground level. These individuals are greatly inconvenienced in a metropolis like New York.

Perhaps the most famous—the most debilitating—phobia is *agoraphobia*. I said a moment ago that it is a fear of open spaces. It might more accurately be described as a *fear of fear*. Agoraphobics stay at home because they can control what happens. They feel safe. They feel in charge. Outside, they're not safe. They're not in charge. They can never be certain that something bad won't happen. Outside their homes, they may fall and hurt themselves. They may get hit by a car. They may get run over by a bus. They may stumble on a robbery in progress. The subway may derail. Someone may fall out of a building and land on them.

I trust you can see how debilitating agoraphobia is. Agoraphobics can't go to work. They can't go to school. They can't go to the supermarket. They can't go to the movies. They're housebound. And that's not a sweet place to be if a person is terrorized to step out the front door.

The origin of phobias depends on the perspective we hold. Currently, the neuroscience and the behavioral perspectives are preferred. The neuroscience perspective asserts that the neurotransmitters serotonin and norepinephrine are the culprits. Anti-anxiety medications aim to raise the level of these medications. The number of such medications grows yearly. To name a few, there's Paxil, Lexapro, Cymbalta, Efflexia, Miltown. Perhaps the most famous is the oldest—Prozac.

The behavioral approach stresses classical conditioning and operant conditioning. In classical conditioning neutral stimuli—innocuous stimuli—get paired with stimuli that are inherently frightening. These neutral stimuli acquire the capacity to produce anxiety. In 1919 the behaviorist John Watson and his future wife Rosalie Rayner performed a notorious experiment on an eleven-month-old child called "Little Albert." The boy was not frightened by a lab rat. Watson and Rayner paired the rat with a stimulus the boy was frightened of—in this case a sudden loud noise. The sudden loud noise served as the unconditioned stimulus resulting in the unconditioned response of fear and anxiety. The rat started out as a neutral stimulus. Paired with the sudden loud noise, the rat came to serve as a conditioned stimulus resulting in the conditioned response of fear and anxiety. The child became frightened of the rat because it was paired with something he was frightened of.

Operant conditioning stresses negative reinforcement as the principle underlying phobias. Negative reinforcement is the situation in which a response removes an unpleasant or aversive stimulus and increases in rate. Phobic individuals learn to avoid the frightening object or situation—they get better and better at this. Sharp objects terrify me—I learn behaviors that avoid sharp objects. Heights terrify me—I learn behaviors that avoid heights. The great outdoors terrify me—I stay at home.

Post-traumatic stress disorder is a heightened response following the experience of trauma. Trauma includes exposure to actual or threatened death, injury, or sexual violence. The trauma may have been personally experienced or witnessed and it may involve hearing the details of an incident experienced by family members or friends.

The heightened response to trauma includes intrusive memories of the incident. The response can include dreams of the incident and *flashbacks*, which are states of confusion in which the person feels as if the traumatic event was reoccurring. There is increased sensitivity to stimuli that resemble events of the trauma. This sensitivity can spread to innocuous stimuli that, like loud noises, occur unexpectedly. The person is hypervigilant and easily aroused and provoked. The person is sensitized and on the verge.

The diagnosis of post-traumatic stress disorder emerged in the Vietnam War era. In earlier wars the condition was called "shell shock." Society recognized that soldiers experience horrible events and need counseling afterward. Post-traumatic stress remains an issue in our time, given that the United States has been at war for more than a decade. The armed services are voluntary, which places excessive burdens on a limited number of people who may endure repeated exposures to terrible events. The numbers vary, but the best estimate is that one in ten combat veterans experiences post-traumatic stress disorder. Given the size of our armed services and the fact that more than two million people have been deployed in Iraq and in Afghanistan since 2001, that adds up to a lot of people who may be in crises.

Post-traumatic stress disorder is not without controversy. Some critics wonder whether it should be included in the DSM. The response to trauma may not be a "disorder." It may be the normal human reaction to the experience of horrific events. Another difficulty that calls the disorder into question is that the pattern of symptoms can occur in people who have not experienced trauma.

Obsessive compulsive disorder use to be categorized as an anxiety disorder, but it now has its own category in the DSM, along with hoarding, as we might expect in a nation that has more than two billion feet of self-storage space. An *obsession is a persistent thought or urge that is unwanted and that causes heightened anxiety.* The person tries to control or reduce these thoughts by other thoughts or by actions. The action is called a *compulsion, which is a repetitive behavior that must be performed in an exact manner.*

I suppose any thought can devolve into an obsession and any behavior constrict into a compulsion. Perhaps the most famous one involves germs. (We can also consider this a germ phobia, which demonstrates the lability of disorders—the same set of symptoms can be called a different disorder.) Individuals are terrified that they will touch something laden with germs or otherwise come into contact with germs. To prevent or undo this possibility, the person engages in compulsions. The person may avoid certain places and engage in excessive hand washing or sanitizing. The person may not shake hands or touch certain objects.

Obsessions and compulsions are caricatures of normal human behaviors. We should take precautions against germs. Banisters in subway stations are sensible things to avoid. I got into a fight with a germ one time and I went down for the ten count. Psychologically disordered individuals take this precaution to a new level when they live their lives around the preoccupation with avoiding germs.

Clinical obsessions and compulsions arise out of ordinary behaviors. We check that we locked the doors to our apartments. We check that we shut electrical appliances off. We hate to discard things. We have superstitions. We feel we must do things in particular ways or bad luck will follow. We have favorite numbers that we play in lotteries. We buy things we do not need and build up vast collections that have to be auctioned off when we go to the big schoolhouse in the clouds. I knew a psychoanalyst—and no, he was not my therapist—who confided that he owned ten thousand books. That is a load of books and bookcases to have in one's home. When it comes time to move, he's going to need a second van. I must have made a face when he told me because he became defensive. He said he thought it was odd to own so many books until he found out that Sigmund Freud owned ten thousand books. That made it all right. It would have been the same story if Sigmund Freud owned ten thousand clothespins. That would have made it all right, too.

The second category of disorder I'll cover is *mood disorders*, which as the name plainly states involve moods and emotions. I'll review two—*major depression* and *bipolar disorder*. The notion of caricature and of exaggeration is clearly seen when we compare ordinary depression with major depression. We've all had days when it hurt to get out of bed. We've all had days when we felt sad and guilty and ashamed. We've all had days in which we felt "blue." We've all had days in which we wanted to throw in the towel and cry "I surrender." Individuals who suffer major depression have more such days and a deeper, more intense and bleaker, mood.

The symptoms of major depression inspire depression. There are feelings of anxiety, guilt, shame, sadness, helplessness and hopelessness. Clinically depressed people don't feel very good about themselves. They see themselves as worthless and unlovable. It's too much of an effort for them to love someone. Depressed people are socially isolated. They don't want to be with people. They can't have a good time. Depressed people have trouble sleeping. They're tired and irritable. They have no motivation and no energy. Things that once delighted them no longer delight them. They have little interest in the daily routine. They are inactive. They cannot get out of the chair. They no longer maintain personal hygiene. Everything—bathing, dressing, preparing meals, changing the channel—is a big deal and a great bother. They may feel pain and physical distress. They feel like they're sick. There may be thoughts of suicide, although that's uncommon in the depths of depression. Ironically, the risk of suicide increases as the depression lifts. It's too much effort to kill oneself when the depression is deepest.

To be diagnosed with major depression, these symptoms have to persist for two weeks or longer.

The cause of major depression depends on the perspective a person holds. The neuroscience perspective suggests that neurotransmitters are the causes, specifically serotonin and norepinephrine. We become depressed when levels of these neurotransmitters lower in the brain. We also become anxious. When the levels rise and return to their normal level, we revert to our usual selves, jovial we hope. The multitude of antidepressant medications work by raising the levels of serotonin and norepinephrine.

Anti-anxiety and antidepressant medications are exceedingly common. There are over two hundred million prescriptions a year written for such medications in the United States. Let me repeat that number—over two hundred million prescriptions a year. This is in a nation of three hundred million. There are controversies with respect to this excessive use of medication. Studies show that medication does not work for every person—I suppose that's true for every medication. In a large 2006 study of three thousand people medicated with antidepressants, the total remission of symptoms occurred in slightly more than one third of the sample. Overall, about a third of the sample relapsed into depression within a year. One third of the sample was not helped at all.

Antidepressant medication and placebos have about the same success rate in relieving depressive symptoms. It may be that both categories of pills work because of the *expectation of recovery*. Experimentally lowering serotonin and norepinephrine levels in non-depressed people does not result in depressive feelings or symptoms. Nor does lowering these neurotransmitters deepen the depression in clinically depressed people. It appears that something else is going on in major depression besides the levels of neurotransmitters. The lowered levels of serotonin and norepinephrine may be collateral elements in a broader causative package. The low levels may be effects of some other process and may not be the causative agents.

The behavioral approach to depression asserts that the depressed individual has lost reinforcements or has experienced excessive punishment. If we add stress to the situation, it's not farfetched to see how a person can slide into a depressed state. We feel overwhelmed and crushed by events. We live hectic lives. We live bruising lives. Sometimes it's easier to stay unwashed and under the blankets than to face another round in the boxing match of daily life.

The social-cultural perspective suggests that depression is the response to the powerlessness people feel in society. This perspective advances this view by noting that depression is more often diagnosed in women than in men. Women experience the feeling of powerlessness more frequently than men. Certainly, there's a huge wage and income gap disparity between women and men. Interestingly, men are more frequently diagnosed as alcoholic than are women. It may be that men conceal their depression through the use of alcohol. And it may be that alcohol use in women is under-diagnosed. Female use of alcohol may be presented as depression. This may be less true in our era of equal rights debauchery and more true in former years in which women had to conceal their drinking. In the old days Grandpa drank openly. His bottle stood proudly on the kitchen counter. Grandma's bottle was hidden in the hamper.

The use of alcohol as a causative factor in depression should not be underestimated. Depressed people drink and drink deepens the depression. Alcohol may make us deliriously happy for a few hours, it may make us superhero brave and Casanova-like cuddly, but in fact alcohol is a depressant and not a stimulant.

The cognitive perspective view of depression has become important in recent years. The concept is that stressful events are interpreted in a pessimistic explanatory style. Depressed people dwell on negative thoughts and engage in dichotomous thinking. Events are only black. Other events are only white. I suppose in a depressed state of mind events are only black and other events are also only black. Depressed people *overgeneralize*—they believe events will always turn out for the worse. Predictions about tomorrow are always gloomy. Depressed people *over-personalize*—they take the blame of their bleak situations to heart. They feel they are responsible for the bad things that happen.

These cognitive tendencies create feelings of helplessness and hopelessness. These tendencies also create a negative cycle that guarantees future causes for depression. Stressful events happen. Depressed people ruminate on them in a negative and self-defeating manner. More stressful events happen. The bad thoughts deepen. Since depressed people believe that things will always be this way and since they believe they are to blame, they start to look for reasons to become depressed. When they experience ambiguous or innocuous events that might otherwise evoke positive conclusions, they draw negative conclusions instead.

We might consider *mood-congruent retrieval* at this point, a concept we covered in the lecture on memory. When people become depressed they start to remember all the other occasions that led to sad and gloomy feelings. The depression may also lead to a reinterpretation of former events. Before the fog of depression settled in, a person had memories that were tinted in shades of happiness or boredom or anger or fear. The depression changes the hue. The memories are now seen as sad and sorrowful.

The bad news is major depression is exceedingly common. Someone called it the "common cold" of serious psychological disorders. I suppose the bad news includes the fact that we have a lot of reasons to be depressed. There's good news, however. Depression is a treatable disorder. Almost anything works. Neuroleptic drugs like Xanax. Placebos. Behavior therapy. Cognitive therapy. Things work that are not considered psychotherapy. Things like treadmills and exercise equipment. Things like Botox. Yes, Botox. The procedure is to inject Botox into the muscles of the face so the person can't frown or make a sad face. Like I said, almost anything works.

An acquaintance once told me that he knew a depressed person who wanted to commit suicide. He said he was sad to hear this, but he would not try to stop the person. He said it was the person's right to take his own life. I disagreed vehemently. Ultimately, it's a personal decision to keep or to leave life, but the decision to end life should not be made in a depressed state. Depression is a state of gloom and doom in which thoughts of suicide all too easily emerge. Depression is a dark state in which counter-arguments against suicide do not easily emerge from the funk. Depression is also a treatable disorder. The depressed person feels hopeless—the light is off at the end of the tunnel—but depression does not have to be a permanent state. If a person wants to end his or her life, that should be a decision made in a state of clear thinking in which hopeful options might be explored. If a person chooses life, that's great. If the person chooses death, well, that's life, too.

Bipolar disorder is a mood disorder that is more striking in symptoms but not as common as major depression. Bipolar disorder involves alternating cycles of major depression and mania. In former years the disorder was called "manic-depressive psychosis." The term *psychosis* refers to the fact that thoughts are not realistic and do not correspond with reality. This happens when the depression and the mania become extreme.

The cycle between the two states varies from person to person. There may be a slow progression from one state to the other. There may be rapid changes from depression into mania and from mania into depression. There may be periods of normal behavior between the depression and the mania. And there are cases in which both depression and mania occur together—the person is depressed in mood and hyperactive and excited in behavior.

The characteristics of mania are the reverse of major depression. In mania there is an elevated and expansive mood. There's an increase in energy and in activity. Activity is disorganized, however. The manic person is distracted and leaps from one task to another. There's an inflated sense of self-worth. The manic person is highly motivated and maintains the attitude that he or she can do anything. It's this unrealistic attitude that propels mania into psychosis. The manic person takes risks and can engage in dangerous and potentially harmful or hurtful behavior. As we might expect, manic individuals are irritable and aggressive. Sometimes they feel they are out of control. Or so they appear to people.

The third category of psychological disorders is the *personality disorders*. These are *long-term and inflexible behavior patterns that impair social functioning*. These patterns are quirks that poison relationships. "Poison" is the right word. Maybe "quirks" is too weak a word. The personality disorders can present intimidating challenges to people.

The *paranoid personality* believes that other people are plotting against him or her. Paranoid personalities suspect that other people are secretly planning to exploit or harm them. They misinterpret innocuous remarks as possessing secret meanings. They are suspicious of anyone who tries to help them. They are not loyal to others and believe that people are not loyal to them. They hold grudges and question the faithfulness of spouses and significant others.

Some years ago I had a student who stopped coming to class. In those days I collected students' phone numbers. In these days I collect students' emails. I called the student and asked why she stopped attending. Was she going to drop the course? She told me that her husband was insanely jealous and refused to allow her to leave their apartment. He was obviously a paranoid type who was highly suspicious of her. I told her this wasn't right and that she had better call the police.

I don't know why she allowed herself to be sealed inside her apartment. Maybe she was frightened of him. Paranoids can be dangerous. Maybe she loved him and thought that she could change him. That's a huge mistake. Paranoids can't be loved and they can't be changed. None of the personality disorders can. None of them can be helped. None of them can be loved to normality. The afflictions are life long and the best response we can make—the safest response—is to sneak out the back door and move to another borough.

Antisocial personality disorder is more famous than the paranoid type. The word "antisocial" does not mean these individuals are not social or that they avoid interacting with people. To the contrary, individuals diagnosed with this disorder often exhibit charm and social graces. They know the rules of the social game. They play the social game very well.

In former days antisocial personalities were called "sociopaths." I don't reckon they liked that term, so it was changed. Before that, sociopaths were called "psychopaths." They liked that term less. A rogue by any name would smell as sour.

Antisocial personalities exhibit a disregard for the rights of others. They often disregard the safety of others. They are deceitful and try to rip people off. They confirm the paranoid's insight and see people as marks ripe for a hustle and a scam. They are the hucksters and the confidence men of the psychiatric world. I suppose I should avoid the charge of sexism and say "confidence people of the psychiatric world" instead.

They do not share the general morality. They lack guilt and remorse when they take advantage of people. They are irresponsible and can be aggressive. They fail to plan ahead and they lack insight into their situation. They don't profit from experience. They live for what attracts them at the moment and they fail to draw the implications of their manipulations. They don't understand that behaviors have consequences, sometimes grave consequences.

So I ask the clerk in the bakery if the last chocolate raspberry linzer on the tray is fresh. It's late afternoon and the pastry has been sweating in the display case since daybreak. A clerk unafflicted with antisocial personality disorder shrugs and points to a different tray. I understand and order something else. This clerk has lost a sale, but gained a customer. A clerk afflicted with antisocial personality disorder cares only about making the sale. He couldn't care less about the consequences of lying to me. He says, "Of course, it's fresh. What'd you think we sell stale pastries?" He probably sounds indignant. As it often is, the joke is on me. I buy the linzer, go home, and crack a tooth on the stale almonds in the dough. The clerk has made a sale, but lost a customer. I'm so annoyed at the dishonesty I'm going to tell all six of my friends about the lousy bakery that sells stale linzers.

As with the paranoid personality type, it's difficult for antisocial personalities to have intimate relationships—honest, sincere, mutually respectful relationships. As with the paranoid personality, it's a major mistake to enter into a relationship with an antisocial personality. Decent and well-meaning people get burned psychologically and the antisocial personality doesn't see what the bother is all about.

Antisocial personalities range from dishonest clerks in bakeries to career criminals and serial killers. The latter are frequently portrayed as cunning villains who outwit bumbling detectives. They are frequently glamorized in books and movies. The truth is anything but. Most serial killers are severely disturbed individuals. They often have substance abuse problems. They often are brain damaged. Their success, if we can call it that, derives from the fact that their crimes mostly target marginal people who have few contacts and who are not missed by the mainstream community. Antisocial personality types can get away with murder, but they can't have an ordinary family life. That's how messed up they are.

The last personality disorder I'll review is ripped from the celebrity headlines. This is the *narcissistic personality*, which is named for Narcissus, a figure in Greek mythology who fell in love with his own reflection. Narcissists have a grandiose sense of their self-importance. They're preoccupied with fantasies of power and success. They're preoccupied with wealth and with physical appearances. They believe they are special and they crave attention. They hate it when they don't get the attention they believe they deserve. They hate you for not giving them any attention. Paranoid personalities see people as targets of lawsuits. Antisocial personalities see people as targets to be ripped off. Narcissists see people as an audience. Their belief is that people are put on this earth to admire and worship them. Of course, it's not the other way around. Narcissists don't admire or worship anyone. They lack reciprocity in relationships. Their attitude is, "You do for me, I do not do for you." Their attitude is "Me first." They're vain, self-centered, and conceited, usually for no special reason.

Narcissists have difficulties forming and staying in relationships. They have no commitment. People are reflective pools for their glorification. People are mirrors in which they can enhance their feelings of self-worth. They like people who like them. They loathe people who ignore them or pay them no mind. They're exploitative of others and full of envy. They hate it when someone else gets more attention. They lack empathy and have little use for people beyond gaining adulation. As with the other personality disorders, it's futile to try to change narcissists. Cure is not possible. The best thing to do with narcissists is to move to another state without leaving a forwarding address.

The final category of psychological disorders I'll review is *thought disorders*, specifically schizophrenia.

Schizophrenia is a serious disorder that affects cognition as well as the emotional and social aspects of a person's life. Schizophrenia includes both active symptoms and passive symptoms.

Perhaps the defining active symptom is the presence of *hallucinations*, which are *false perceptions*. The perceptions may involve touch, in which the person feels unusual sensations in the body, and smell, in which the person smells odors that are not real or present to the sense. I knew a man who suffered olfactory hallucinations. He kept asking if I smelled a particular odor. "Do you smell it, man?" he asked in a thick Jamaican accent. I said that I did and that to me it smelled like mothballs. He didn't believe me.

The most common source of hallucinations in schizophrenia involves the sense of hearing—*auditory hallucinations*. Schizophrenics do not ordinarily see things—visual hallucinations involve brain damage. Schizophrenics hear voices. At first, the voices are whispers. In fact, there's an excellent book about auditory hallucinations called *Whispers* by Ronald Siegel. The whispers increase in volume and they grow so loud and so insistent they can drown out the world's noises, which in your country is saying something. The voices can be so loud and so intimidating, the person freezes in terror. This freezing is called *catatonia* and it can involve odd positions. Sometimes the person talks back to the voices and reacts to them in an agitated manner.

Schizophrenia is an example of a disorder that involves psychosis. In psychosis the thinking process does not match reality. We can note this with regard to auditory hallucinations. The voices are not present in reality. No one else hears them. The voices can come through walls and through furniture. They can come through animals and through plants. They can come from outer space. They can come from the interior of the earth. Schizophrenics have an inkling the voices are not physically real, but they are not certain. The voices may be inside their heads. The voices may be outside their heads. They don't know which. The voices perplex them mightily.

The hallucinations are telling the schizophrenic *delusions*, which are *false beliefs*. Delusions also represent psychotic thinking, although they can be more subtle than hallucinations. No one has any trouble hearing the psychotic element in a statement like "My wife is from another dimension." The psychotic element in a statement like "My wife is a witch" is more difficult to ascertain.

There are broad categories of delusions. *Delusions of reference* involve the false belief that events in reality refer to oneself. The schizophrenic hears laughter in the hallway—he believes people are laughing at him. The schizophrenic hears footsteps—he believes someone is coming to get him. The schizophrenic sees two people conversing across from him on the uptown IRT—he believes they're talking about him. Probably, he gets off at the next stop.

Delusions of persecution are exactly that. The schizophrenic believes people are out to get him and that there are plots against him. When delusions of persecution are prevalent in the disorder we speak of *paranoid schizophrenia*. These delusions can cause a life to grind to a halt. They can also lead to trouble if the schizophrenic acts on the beliefs. I saw a cartoon once—all right, it was in *Mad* magazine. A paranoid schizophrenic is walking on a street somewhere in suburbia. He says, "I don't see anyone hiding." He continues walking. In the next frame he says, "I better take my gun out." He takes his gun out and continues walking. In the last frame he says, "I still don't see anyone, but I better spray the neighborhood with bullets to be on the safe side." Fortunately, no one drops out of the bushes. I guess you had to see the cartoon to think it was funny.

Delusions of persecution offer little reason for approbation. They're no reason to place a notice in the newspaper. But they are difficult to change. For starters, they don't match reality. It's difficult to correct what doesn't exist—I should say what doesn't exist outside the schizophrenic's mind. In addition, the delusions provide explanations for the schizophrenic's woes. "My life is troubled because they've been plotting against me." "I haven't advanced in life because they've been poisoning me." "I'm lonely because they've been tampering with the water supply." "I'm tormented because cosmic rays are coming through the hot water pipes."

Delusions of grandeur involve the false beliefs that a person is special or possesses some unique talent or unique fate. In a sense delusions of grandeur provide the rationale for the delusions of persecution. "They're persecuting me because I am someone special," the schizophrenic thinks. Like the rest of us, the schizophrenic runs into a problem at this point. He doesn't possess a unique talent. So far, there's no hint of a unique fate. So the schizophrenic has to make one up—or one has to be made up for him—that does not correspond with reality. The reason a person is being persecuted does not accord with the way things are.

The interpersonal psychiatrist Harry Stack Sullivan did a lot of work with schizophrenics in the 1920s and claimed to be schizophrenic himself or to have had some type of psychological crises when he was a young man. No one living knows for sure whether Sullivan was or wasn't schizophrenic, but his work in the 1920s is certainly well documented. Sullivan suggested that *the central feature in schizophrenia is a loss of control of awareness.* The schizophrenic has lost control of an aspect of his mind. As it were, a fragment of the mind splits off—hence, the term "schizophrenia," which is Greek for "split mind." The splitting happens at the psychological moments when hallucinations and delusions occur.

Schizophrenics are not multiple personalities, whatever they may be, and they have not suffered the eruption of repressed thoughts and wishes into consciousness as psychoanalysts once suggested. If anything, schizophrenic individuals know all too well what's going on in their minds. They just can't make sense of what's happening with their thought processes.

Sullivan gave an interesting example of what it feels like to be schizophrenic. This example has helped me because, as I keep telling everyone, I'm perfectly normal. Before I give the example I have to preface it with a little self disclosure to provide context and a comparison. When I was in high school I had a crushingly boring history teacher. Some teachers make history come alive. This teacher made history die. He read from his notes in a flat and nasal tone of voice. His voice never changed in tone or in volume. His voice never showed the least emotion, not even when it narrated doom and destruction on a national scale.

"The battle of Gettysburg was fought in Adams County, Pennsylvania, from July 1 to July 3," he said in starting. The class dragged on and on for the next forty two minutes. Since he never asked questions or noted if anyone paid attention, I immediately traveled in mind to fantasy land. This was to a place that resembled Pensacola, Florida. Pinching hot sand underfoot. Green water. Blue clouds studded with wisps of pure white cumulus. Girls in skimpy bikinis rubbing sunscreen on. Cold beer and warms franks in the stand on the boardwalk. Or was it warm beer and cold franks? In any event, you get the idea. Fantasy land was pleasant for me. I could start it and stop it at will. Strangely, it ended the moment the word "quiz" was uttered in a flat and nasal voice. I could change the details. I understood the particulars. I understood which was reality and which was fantasy.

This is not what happens in schizophrenia. The fantasies of schizophrenics are not pleasant. Schizophrenics don't like experiencing them. They can't start the fantasies—they don't want to start them. They can't stop them. They can't change them. They don't understand what's going on. They don't understand the particulars. They're not sure which is reality and which is not.

Onto Sullivan's example. It's night and we're asleep and dreaming. It's an impressive dream and brilliantly vivid. We're on a beach. The endless ocean is ahead of us. The endless sky is above us. Vast gray mountains are behind us. Blades of sunlight agitate the surf. Dolphins leap from the water and cavort in the air. Suddenly, the dream starts to turn bad. We know we're on the verge of a nightmare. We know something bad is about to happen. We promptly wake up. For a few seconds we know we're awake, but the dream continues as if we were asleep. We're in two psychological places at once. We're awake and, simultaneously, we're dreaming. We're awake and the dream is proceeding on its own accord. According to Sullivan, this is what it feels like to be schizophrenic.

The non-schizophrenic gets up and goes to the bathroom. I'm sure the sound of a toilet flushing has prevented many the incipient psychosis. The schizophrenic experiences this mental splitting in broad daylight and while wide awake. This splitting can happen on the train. It can happen in the classroom. It can happen at the bakery counter. And as noted, this loss of control of awareness does not lead to a pretty place.

The loss of control of awareness may account for the passive or negative symptoms of schizophrenia, which include flat emotionless moods and social withdrawal. Schizophrenics are preoccupied with making sense of perplexing and terrifying mental states. They're confused to the cores of their beings. It follows that they're not particularly convivial. I don't suspect that anyone would be in a jovial mood if they understood that a portion of their minds could derail and lead them into a mental wreck. Schizophrenics are walking on cognitive egg shells and this state is not conducive to cheery conversations at checkout counters.

The loss of control of awareness may also account for the, at times, unusual use of language demonstrated by schizophrenics. Schizophrenics are sometimes incoherent and they sometimes use words differently than the rest of us. The words they use may not mean the same to us as it does to them. The connotations of their words are not consensual, so to say. We don't share the same meanings of the words. We can't follow their train of thought. It doesn't make sense to us. We're not exactly sure what they mean. I suppose they share the same predicament. They're not exactly sure what they mean.

There are two broad avenues leading to schizophrenia. The first is called *process schizophrenia*. These individuals never caught onto how to be social. When you think of it, being social—being successfully social—takes a lot of work and requires a lot of skill and information. We need to know what to say and when to say it. We have to get ourselves understood by other people, especially by people we want to be intimate with. Sometimes that's not an easy task. For whatever reason, process schizophrenics have failed in this task. Maybe the failure is genetic. Maybe it involves a thus far undiscovered brain defect. Maybe it's simpler than that. Whatever it is, they live increasingly isolated lives. They become preoccupied with fantasies and with their interior lives—maybe their hallucinations resemble the beach in Pensacola rather than the beach in our nightmares. They find it impossible to communicate their thoughts. We find it impossible to understand their communications. When we make the attempt and can't understand the gist of what a person is saying, we give up trying. When people can't communicate the stories of their lives—when people can't say what's on their minds—they give up trying. The social isolation increases. Process schizophrenics step to the side and fade out of the world of social interaction.

The other avenue into schizophrenia involves stress. It's called *reactive* or *acute schizophrenia* and it's a stormy and hectic path. Euphemistically, reactive schizophrenia is called a *nervous breakdown*. It not infrequently happens in young people—in teens and young adults. Schizophrenia was, in fact, previously called *dementia praecox*—dementia of the young. Interestingly, the majority of psychological disorders begin to manifest in people before they're in the mid-twenties.

As you might recall from the lecture on health psychology, there are many sources of stress. Financial concerns, interpersonal concerns, health concerns, concerns about school, concerns about sex and about sexual orientations—these stressors accumulate and overwhelm a person. In individuals so predisposed, a fragment of their mind splits under the stress. They lose control of awareness and experience hallucinations.

At this point the questions are, "What happens now?" and "What happens next?" If schizophrenic individuals seek psychological help or if they are forced to seek it, they will receive psychiatric medications. These medications are called "major tranquilizers" for good reason. They put the person to sleep. As the person sleeps, the stressors disappear. Their loans are forgiven. Their significant others have moved out of state. Their health improves. They've failed the course. Their sexual urges are sedated. In a manner of speaking, their problems were solved as they slept.

When they wake up—when their medication is adjusted to a level in which they can function—they can get a fresh start. In the ideal situation the person can learn to handle and to avoid stress. Psychiatric medications will not "cure" the person. Medication slows the thought processes so that the hallucinations become manageable. Medication is insufficient to bring about change unless the sources of stress are identified and eliminated. This takes counseling and therapy and education. This takes a lot of work and an understanding environment that cooperates with the person.

I want to stress that schizophrenia is not necessarily the Bowling Green of psychological disorders—that's the last stop on the subway in the great Borough of Manhattan. Many individuals recover from their "nervous breakdowns." Many do not, but still lead productive and creative lives. Schizophrenia is something in the human experience. However distressful it may be, it is a way to be human. Anxious individuals, depressed individuals, individuals afflicted with personality disorders, and schizophrenic individuals—they are more than the labels attached to their conditions. They are something different than their conditions and they are something greater. We should never forget this fact.

Thank you.

Tips to Students ~
How Do You Fill Time?

This is a key question—what do you fill your time doing?

This is a key insight—whatever you fill your time doing will *exclude* everything else from your life.

This is another key question—what are you *excluding* from your life by filling time doing the things you do?

These questions and this insight are relevant in every area of our lives. What are we filling time doing that excludes—*prevents*—engaging in social activities? In creative activities? In health-promoting activities? In economically-stimulating activities? In intellectual activities? And, apropos of this course, in educational activities?

It may be a profitable experience to review how we fill time in ways that prevent us from studying. What are we doing that excludes reading the textbook and reviewing the class notes and thinking about the subject matter of the course? What are we doing that excludes homework? What are we doing that excludes elaborative rehearsal of the content of the course?

Once we become aware of how we fill time and of what we are excluding, it may be easier to adjust our priorities and to exchange one task for another. Reading and studying and reviewing class notes and thinking about the course can now exclude the behaviors we once engaged in. These behaviors may be important and maybe they can't be excluded, but they may be superficial and trifles that stand in the way of obtaining better grades. The decision is ours—what is important at this moment in our day and what can be excluded to our betterment?

A Note on the Choice of the Cover Photograph

People who saw the cover photograph before the book was published remarked that it was bright and cheery and somewhat out of place in a dense intellectual tome. I suppose these people preferred a photograph of Rodin's *Thinker* or a photograph of the *Pensive Christ* that's carved in wood and sold in flea markets in Baltic old towns. I felt I needed to give an explanation for the choice of the photograph.

The photograph, which was taken some years ago in Oahu, provides the opportunity to speculate about the personality of the surfer. Who is he? What's his name? Where's he from? How old is he? What kind of person is he? Is he a friendly guy? Or is he unfriendly?—he's alone, after all. Can he surf? Or is he a poseur who strolls the beach board in hand, giving people the impression that he surfs when, in fact, he doesn't? Is he a tourist? Or is he a resident of Oahu? Did he go to college? If he did, what was his major? What does he do for a living? Does he have a job? Or is he a proverbial beach bum, living splendidly in the great outdoors? Does he have a girlfriend? Is he married? Does he have a family? Does he have siblings? Do they surf? Where do his parents live? What do his parents do for a living? We can go on with these questions all day long. If we were adherents of the psychodynamic perspective, we might supply answers to these questions through the accommodating process of projection.

The photograph allows us to progress from considering the particulars of an individual life to speculating about the psychological principles covered in Volume Two. We can consider this solitary surfer in the light of Lecture One on sleep and dreams. In a REM dream he's pursued by shrieking great whites looking to swallow him whole. In a NREM dream he's tumbled off the board into shallow water in full view of tourists.

We can consider the surfer using the principles outlined in Lecture Two on motivation. We assume he's surfing for the positive reinforcement he gains and for purposes of intrinsic motivation—he surfs for the sheer fun and excitement of catching a big wave. And we assume that surfing satisfies the five levels of Maslow's hierarchy of needs.

The principle of adaptation level presented in Lecture Three on emotions indicates that the surfer's happiness increases as he gets better at surfing. The principle of relative deprivation indicates that his happiness increases as he glides amid a school of novices riding boogie boards in the shallow water. Feedback from the face modulates the emotions. The fear face increases the fear that the crest of a two story wave is about to drop on his board. The happiness face increases the happiness that the crest is about to drop behind him out of harm's way.

Our surfer looks like he inhabits the land of wellness. We like to think he manages stress in terms of the variables reviewed in Lecture Four on health psychology and stress. He knows when the water's gentle and when the waves turn into monsters that gobble the shoreline and everything on it. We can assume his coping style is active-behavioral and we can assume the surfer has the belief he can control events once the sea starts rolling.

We can consider the surfer using the principles of social psychology reviewed in Lecture Five. We want to avoid making the fundamental attribution error in the surfer's case. He wants to avoid this error, too, but he may not want to avoid the self-serving bias, as he credits his successful rides to his skill and blames the wrath of Neptune for his spills. If he sees himself as competent, he'll proceed to a crowded beach—maybe that's where he's going. If he sees himself as incompetent, he may stay on the lonely beach where he is. Since the beach is mostly deserted, he can expect our help in the event that something goes awry.

We are in no position to consider the surfer through the concepts expressed in Lecture Six on psychological disorders. We don't know him well enough—we don't know him at all. Keeping the difficulties of diagnosis in mind, we can't say whether riding the barrel of a maverick is normal or abnormal behavior. If the surfer is afflicted with any disorder, it would likely be with a personality disorder or with an anxiety disorder. It takes a little narcissism to stroll on a beach in bathing trunks carrying a surfboard. A few wipe outs in stormy waters could eventuate in a phobia or in post-traumatic stress.

From a single individual in a photograph we traverse a fertile ocean teeming with inquiries. There's another reason I chose this photograph for the cover. A 2008 study by Berman, Jonides and Kaplan entitled *Cognitive Benefit of Interacting with Nature* found that people who looked at photographs of nature while performing difficult intellectual chores exercised greater cognitive control in comparison to a control group that looked at photographs of crowded urban scenes.

Amid the strenuous mental task of contemplating these lectures, readers can fold the corner of the page, close the book, and daydream about surfing the North Shore of Oahu. Or, if you're like me, readers can daydream of watching someone surf the North Shore of Oahu. Our minds, if only temporarily, shift from dry intellectual pursuits to the possibility of hanging ten on a waxed deck in the warm white surf of Sunset Beach. Properly refreshed, we can reopen the book, fold back the page, and rejoin a voyage that has brought so many psychological marvels into our reckoning.

Printed in the United States
By Bookmasters